To:
Rich & Dolores Keyes
Flahrin & Vivian McKay
1/25/13

D1524447

EBB TIDE:
Nancy Astor's Greatest Challenge

Copyright© 2008 Dr. J. Calvin McCray

Permission to reproduce any part of this book
must be obtained in writing from
Dr. J. Calvin McCray
jcmccray@comcast.net

This book is a work of non-fiction. Names, characters, places and incidents actually existed and took place at specified times; any misrepresentations of incidents occurred are unintentional.

Published by G Publishing, LLC
P. O. Box 24374
Detroit, MI 48224

ISBN 13: 978-0-9814650-9-8
ISBN 10: 0-9814650-9-9

Library of Congress Control Number: 2008931452

Printed in the United States of America

EBB TIDE:

Nancy Astor's

Greatest Challenge

Dr. J. Calvin McCray

TABLE OF CONTENTS:

PHOTOGRAPHS AND ILLUSTRATIONS:

FOREWORD

I received my Fulbright Award fifty years ago in the Spring of 1958, amid the struggles of the Civil Rights Movement (particularly the Little Rock school crisis). Since then, the racial and cultural problems in America, in many respects, have not improved. Some cities and many schools are still divided by race, although Federal Troops are no longer needed to integrate the schools.

The challenges facing America today are even more serious than the clash between black and white. They confront us as a nation on a worldwide cultural level.

The Fulbright Program has greatly intensified its efforts in the past fifty years, realizing that society (in America, and globally) is enveloped in a war of cultures. Fulbrighters, who meet people and participate in cultures abroad, return home with knowledge they can use to help us understand people from all parts of the globe.

My optimism for the Fulbright Program is as strong today as it was when Lady Nancy Astor emphasized the necessity for my wife Vivian and me to share our American values with the rest of the world.

My values were shaped by my childhood on the south side of Chicago and by my experiences with racial integration in school and the community and segregation in universities and the Armed Services. All of those things are part of what this book intends to share with its readers.

Vivian and I received an unbelievable exchange of life experiences with a person of exceptional international and historical acclaim (whom we knew simply as Nancy). She helped propel our intercultural experience to another level. I cannot help but celebrate her as an extraordinary individual who touched our lives.

PROLOGUE

This book was approximately fifty years in the making. That gestation period provided me ample time to reflect and accumulate my notes from fading files, photos, and memories.

I grew up in Chicago during the Great Depression, World War II, and the 1950's.

Those years, however troubling, were only a preparation for the years to come.

The years following World War II provided growth and prosperity. There was a corresponding increase in racial tension in America as black people strove to gain their rightful piece of the American pie. That turbulent time was intertwined with my educational and social growth.

At Indiana University in 1951, I learned about the Fulbright Program, in its infancy at that time. My former Dean, Harold Shane, encouraged me to apply. (I had studied School Curriculum and Administration under him at Northwestern University before he came to Indiana in 1950.)

The program had no prerequisites regarding race and thus did not discriminate against me because of the color of my skin. I sought to become part of it. My hard work eventually paid off, and I was admitted to the program in 1958.

Having earned the honor of being a Fulbright Scholar, I was provided an early opportunity that would eventually lead to learning about many cultures abroad.

This book is about some of the people who helped me initiate and continue on my educational journey, a journey that continues to this day. All my "fellow travelers" were instrumental in shaping me—some to a greater extent than others—but all in some significant way. In my life, I was very lucky to have known a number of celebrities—famous people of various accomplishments (E.R. Braithwaite, Alex Haley, Drs. Robert and Virginia Lewis, Jack Dempsey, John M. Timken, the Queen

Mother, and many others). They all contributed to making me what I am today by allowing me to synthesize and pull together the significant pieces of my life to make it what I wanted it to be.

As important as each person was, one of them stood out. My education journey began in earnest when I met perhaps the most dynamic person I've had the pleasure to know in a lifetime of meeting dynamic people. Lady Astor, or Nancy, was the light that turned me on to see the tunnel ahead and broadened my point of view as I exited the other end.

For one year (1958-1959), Nancy Langhorne Astor shared her life with two American teachers—my wife, Vivian, and me, James Calvin McCray. The Civil Rights Laws of 1964-65 had not yet been passed; so much of what we discussed concerned the struggles for freedom of African Americans during that time. Those conversations, and her friendship, are something that I treasure and will never forget.

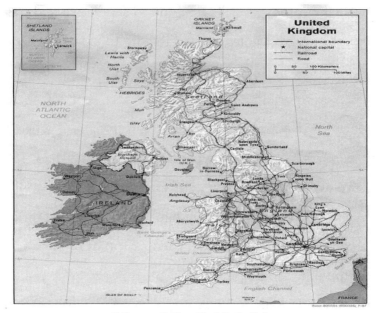

Map of the British Isles

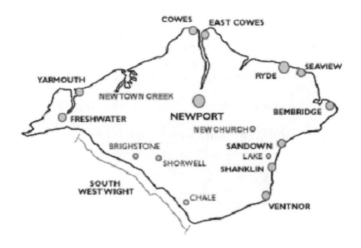

Map of the Isle of Wight

Part One:

Meeting Nancy

Lady Astor, painted by John Singer Sargent in 1909.

THE WHITE HOUSE
WASHINGTON

Dear Fellow Citizen:

You have been issued a valued credential – the Passport of the United States. It requests that, in the countries you intend to visit, there be provided you, as an American citizen, safe passage, lawful aid and protection in case of need. As the holder of this passport, you will be the guest of our neighbors and friends in the world family of nations.

Year after year, increasing numbers of our citizens travel to foreign countries. In most of these lands there exist a reservoir of good will for the United States and a knowledge of what we stand for. In some areas, our country and its aspirations are less well understood. To all the varied peoples of these many countries, you, the bearer of an American passport, represent the United States of America.

As you travel abroad, the respect you show for foreign laws and customs, your courteous regard for other ways of life, and your speech and manner help to mold the reputation of our country. Thus, you represent us all in bringing assurance to the people you meet that the United States is a friendly nation and one dedicated to the search for world peace and to the promotion of the well-being and security of the community of nations.

Sincerely,

Dwight D. Eisenhower

S. S. United States

Chapter 1:

S.S. United States

On June 6, 1958, I received my final approval from the Department of State to teach in the United Kingdom.

I was one of a hundred American teachers selected to teach in the British Isles through the Fulbright Program of International Education and Cultural Exchange.

I had two months to make last-minute plans. August came, and we embarked. There were tons of people present; I was just one in a million.

The people aboard the ship were all excited and eager for the adventure ahead. Though some of the two thousand passengers appeared exhausted and apprehensive to be leaving their cherished homes, it was obvious that they were still happily embracing the journey. The destination probably didn't matter at the time.

I had not thought about it then, but, reminiscing about the situation on the docks in New York Harbor, I realize that there were no other blacks, that I could see, boarding the S.S United States. I saw a few among the crowd, waving goodbye, but my wife, Vivian, and I were the only ones, it seemed, who boarded. We had been married for seven years at that point and had both been teaching for as long as we'd been together.

It is quite an experience for anyone to visit a ship's departure, especially as grand and vast a ship as the one we found ourselves boarding. From the docks with the hull looming above, one could not see the top of the ship's smoke stacks nor see from the bow to the stern.

I was familiar with many ships from my time in the Coast Guard during World War II, but none delighted me like this one; it was the finest ship that I had ever seen. In fact, my Coast Guard vessel ("Cutter" class) could have fit entirely and inconspicuously on this ship's bow.

Someone in the crowd behind us was reciting some unbelievable statistics—e.g., "She's 17 stories tall, with 19 elevators"; "She can carry two thousand passengers." At that point the numbers seemed astronomical. "The Big U," as she was known, was famous for being the preferred transport of Heads of State, such as President Eisenhower and various celebrities.

It was an hour past noon when we finally boarded, gaining relief from the blazing sun. Our departure from New York Harbor seemed to take forever.

I watched several tiny tug-boats coming to nudge the huge liner out into the New York Harbor.

Passengers cheered at the sight of the Great Lady with the torch. Many had seen the Statue of Liberty before, as they, or their families, had come to Staten Island as immigrants.

I could understand their happiness and reminders of their American heritage. I couldn't imagine how my ancestors arrived in the United States, or perhaps I didn't want to imagine it—as their means of travel was a slave ship and their likely destination was Virginia, farther south than Staten Island.

I wanted to find a good spot on deck and relax as soon as possible. After all, it had been a busy day.

*   *   *

Vivian and I arrived for the orientation in New York City a couple of days earlier than planned to take in the notable sights. During World War II, I had seen the

Empire State Building, Times Square, and the Waldorf-Astoria among other sights while stationed in the Coast Guard at Manhattan Beach in Brooklyn, N.Y. It had been fifteen years since my military service, and the country was enjoying a time of prosperity and peace. The sight-seeing proved tiring, but we believed several days relaxing aboard the ship would satisfy our restless bodies.

The school where I was teaching in Gary, IN had been out on vacation for the summer of 1958 and I had spent most of it preparing for my trip to England. Prior to my Fulbright selection, I taught in both the Gary and Chicago Public School Systems.

Vivian had prepared herself mentally by reconciling herself to not teaching and accepting the challenge to make the year as pleasant and educational as possible. She looked forward to new acquaintances and exploring the cultural environment in the Isle of Wight.

The group had met a day before departure at New York University to hear lectures from Fulbright Officials and former Fulbright Scholars who had been to the British Isles. These were stimulating sessions. Our final session was a panel on international and cultural relations. It was to assure that we would all handle our situations abroad judiciously and as informed American citizens.

Earlier that same day, August 8, 1958, Vivian and I had spent two hours visiting Fidel Castro who occupied the suite on the floor above us at the Hotel Theresa in Harlem.

We had gotten up early that morning, having stayed the night, to have breakfast in the dining room and then take a taxi to the pier by noon. Our luggage had been shipped the day before, so we had only carry-on luggage to prepare.

Several Latino men were ordering large quantities of food to be sent to their room. Inquisitively I asked if they were visitors. Their English was good, but they spoke in Spanish to each other. New York was their last stop before heading to Havana, they said, grinning delightedly. The group seemed somewhat annoyed by the service they were receiving from the hotel staff, but, even so, they were friendly and talkative.

They invited us upstairs to their room. We followed them, up the elevator and down the hall, not intending to visit with them for very long. When we entered the suite, there seemed to be a casual party going on, with a dozen other fellow Cubans bustling around a man who seemed to be in the center of it all, a bearded man whom I recognized from newspaper photographs: Fidel Castro.

There he stood, lacking his now typical forest-green fatigues but sporting his characteristic beard. This was his first visit to the United States, and it was during the heated days of his revolution alongside Ernesto "Che" Guevara, against Cuba's military leader Fulgencio Batista.

In our brief conversation, Castro spoke passionately, explaining his adversarial position toward U.S. influence on Cuba's affairs. I told him about my career as an elementary-school teacher and that Vivian and I had both obtained our Master's degrees from Indiana University. He spoke of his Law degree and how he had been a candidate for a seat in the Cuban parliament in 1952; those political aspirations were dashed by the military coup of Fulgencio Batista that resulted in the cancellation of the election. I gathered from Mr. Castro, since his nationalism was just as strong the day I met him as it had ever been, that Batista's coup was the last straw, so to speak.

Hardly four years later, after meeting this man on friendly terms at the Hotel Theresa, we heard about the

Cuban missile crisis. At the time, I thought how he and I had come close to establishing a legitimate friendship. He even asked us to visit Cuba when we returned from England. Before I knew it, two hours had passed; we were lucky to get to the ship on time.

*   *   *

The passengers were anxious and restless for adventure. Some of them had never set eyes on the open sea and were eager for the sight. It was the experience of a lifetime. Some of the faces I saw also expressed an anxiety over sea travel; maybe they feared reaching the other side or anticipated sea sickness.

Exploring this ship, with all its vastness, might have been like a week-end in my hometown Chicago. Certainly this ship was a place for dreamers.

Although the American Fulbrights were invariably from cultures all around the world, we didn't notice anyone else of color. We heard that there were people of great wealth aboard who were mingling about and participating in various ship activities. They looked as ordinary as the tourists.

The journey from New York to England aboard the S.S. United States would last four days. I found the experience to be extremely calming and a lot of fun. Everyone was enthusiastic, and it was an opportunity to meet new friends. I spent much of my time strolling along the upper deck, gazing out at the vast blue sea, and reminiscing on my own experiences in school as I thought more and more about all the new people I would soon be meeting and teaching in another country.

Occasionally while striding along the deck and exploring the ship I would encounter a fellow Fulbright. We would nod and smile at one another, maybe exchange a few brief words of introduction and our own anxiety about the responsibilities that lay ahead. I had yet to encounter another Fulbright with dark skin.

During this trip, we met many people from British Commonwealth countries, such as Juan and Pauline Bunting, who were from Jamaica.

The Buntings were the first and only people of color that we met aboard. We had dinner with them that night and afterwards saw the movie *That Certain Smile*, starring Rossano Brazzi and Johnnie Mathis. I still sing "That Certain Smile" even today because it helps remind me of that fateful journey.

The good life aboard the S.S. United States began the second day, after everyone was supposed to have rested from the tiring welcoming ceremonies. The ship was like a grand hotel—the Waldorf-Astoria, perhaps.

It was before dawn on the last day at sea when it was announced over the intercom that the islands on our starboard side were the Isles of Scilly, the southern most part of the United Kingdom; Land's End was on our port side, and we would arrive at Southampton in four hours. Practically everyone in the dining room let out a happy yell. Vivian and I yelled along with the rest, some of whom were Fulbrighters, probably happy that the voyage, however magnificent, was finally nearing its destination.

Shortly before noon after four wonderful days at sea, the grand ship came to a virtual halt awaiting assistance to enter its special terminal at Southampton. I gazed out at the Isle of Wight lying on our starboard side.

The ship's loudspeaker blasted embarkation instructions and announcements welcoming us to England and informing the passengers that the voyage had been made in record time. Among the announcements, the voice blared, "American black to teach in the British Isles."

Scenes on the Isle of Wight

We didn't need an announcement over the ship's intercom to inform listeners we were black. It was quite obvious; we were easily distinguished among the sea of white faces. It wasn't that we were to teach in England, but rather the fact that we were black that mattered. The terminology "Black" was not used in the United States at that time but was typical inside British Colonial countries.

We took the ill-advised announcement to be positive. Maybe the ship's management thought that this announcement was good news, to be celebrated by the majority of passengers or the visitors who were listening in the reception area.

"Did you hear that announcement?" I nudged Vivian. The loud, disembodied voice had effectively thrown a spotlight on the two of us. People began to gather around us, and we were suddenly encircled by a large group of greeters, congratulating all of the arriving Fulbright Scholars, particularly me. They wanted to know more about the two of us and where we would be teaching. Among those descending from the S.S. United States, our group of Americans coming to teach in the British Isles was the largest.

The sky was a radiant blue without a cloud in sight, and the unforgiving August sun made me perspire as we waited on the docks. People of many backgrounds and cultures continued to gather and greet one another. It felt good to be among the crowd of happy people, regardless of the punishing weather. Though weary from a half-week's travel, I made sure all of our personal belongings were securely stacked along the ship's bulkhead.

It was well past noon on August 13, 1958, when we finally cleared customs and entered the terminal area designated for sea arrivals. We were among several hundred people arriving in England that day.

Our group of a hundred Fulbrights from America would exchange with a counterpart from the British Isles: for every American teacher who entered an English classroom, an English teacher would take his place in an American classroom. My counterpart's name was Cyril Doughty, a teacher in the East Cowes County junior school in the Isle of Wight.

Twenty feet away, I recognized a woman swiveling through a crowd of animated friends and visitors, hugging one another. It was Nancy Astor, or Lady Astor, as she was now known, the first woman to serve as a member of the British Parliament. Her political career had ended with her retirement from office in 1945. Lady Astor was in her mid-seventies but looked years younger. Certainly, she was sprightly and graceful and full of energy. She wore two rows of pearls around her neck. Her earrings were one-piece circular and clearly visible as her hair was brushed back on the nape of her neck. Her eyes still maintained the bluish tint of yesterday but seemed clearer and more intense.

This stunningly dressed woman had a glow in her eyes that assured me she knew where she was headed and for whom she was looking. She approached the two of us and came to a sudden stop. "You are the McCrays aren't you?" she asked.

Chapter 2:

Nancy's Private Car

This was no coincidence; she had been waiting for us. As part of the welcoming committee, Nancy knew that a black teacher was coming to the British Isles.

I straightened my tie and took a breath.

"Yes, we are the McCrays," I said. "I am Cal, and this is my wife, Vivian."

"I received a wire photo of you two boarding ship three days ago and knew to expect you," she said in a definitive voice.

We each extended our hands to Lady Astor.

"Please call me Nancy...and welcome to England," she said.

We gasped for words for a second or two, as if we had frogs in our throats.

She was radiantly attired in a tailored light-beige Edwardian dress, the hem three to four inches below the knees, as was the custom at that time. She carefully removed her wide-brim hat, revealing the length of her hair, falling slightly above her shoulders, displaying the blonde of her earlier days amongst the streaks of silver.

Nancy's exquisite style of dress was more elegant than that of everyone else waiting to greet the new arrivals. As we would have said about a woman's appearance in our culture, "She was really sharp!"

Still feeling the fatigue of a long journey, we were a bit startled by this sudden but pleasant greeting from this sprightly lady.

"Did you hear that announcement?" I asked Nancy, still feeling bothered by it.

"Don't take that negatively," Nancy said, the hum of dozens of other people being greeted helped keep our conversation private. "The eyes were on you, so take it honorably. You were the only one that was singled out. When you walked down that gangplank your blackness was representing a cause."

Nancy knew that I was equating being called "black" with discrimination in America, but this situation was not the case.

"Thanks, Nancy," I said. I appreciated her understanding and explained to her that, every day, in some form or other, the color of my skin reminded me of the looming problem of race in the United States.

As we briefly held hands, it felt as though we had met before—maybe in Times Square or perhaps on North Michigan Avenue in Chicago. I looked down at Nancy's hands, much smaller than mine and contrasting in color.

She took pleasure in the two of us, and the feeling was mutual. I frequently became a bit defensive, at least initially, every time Nancy made an utterance, but I also felt that she completely understood my reactions.

*   *   *

Our next mode of travel would be by train.

As Nancy led the way up the train steps, one could see that her shoes—a light tan of upscale fashion—were gracefully matching both her outfit and her zippered shoulder handbag. The light-blue band on her beige hat somehow shared the same tint of blue in her eyes. She often looked back as we followed her, flashing the most charismatic smile and drifting along with the grace and softness of falling snow.

We followed, not knowing where we were being led. She seemed to know where she was going, as no one was there to assist her.

"This is my private car," she said, waving her hand lazily toward the large train segment sitting before us. She still had a strict sophistication in her demeanor, but it seemed to have been relaxed over the years. Her earnestness was charming and infectious.

Her own private car! I thought to myself, mightily impressed.

Nancy's private car was similar to a studio room, with seats permanently arranged for sitting and sleeping. The room was immaculate, precisely ordered in every detail, and seemed to have been prepared especially for her. It was first class.

Once we entered Nancy's compartment and slid the door shut, we were alone, finally separated from the crowd that still lingered out on the platform. We were relieved to be out of the unusually hot sun and looked forward to a comfortable seat and a chance to stretch out.

We weren't quite comfortable with each other yet. We were still getting to know each other, still feeling each other out. Nancy complimented Vivian's dress, a three-piece outfit with three-quarter-length turtleneck blouse that had two white bands at the neck and waist.

Vivian thanked her, self-consciously revealing that she hadn't had time to change before the ship docked.

"I know how you must feel after a long voyage such as that," Nancy sympathized. "I've traveled this same route many times on the Aquatania and Olympia and the Cedric—it took 11 days, and I enjoyed it more each time."

My journey had only taken 3 days, 14 hours and 40 minutes, and yet she was commiserating with us.

"We're not exhausted," said Vivian, "just a bit

exasperated. Every event on that ship was a drama, and it felt as if I were on stage most of the time, even during the life-boat drill."

Morning safety drills on the S.S. U. S.

Every morning aboard the S.S. United States, we had had a safety drill. Even at that late date, there were British sailors still deathly cautious from the memory of the Titanic's tragedy—safety was of the utmost concern.

"Now that excitement is passing," I said, "we're ready to settle down and seek new adventure."

After the rest of the Fulbright group boarded, a large shudder reverberated throughout the train, and the steady chug of the locomotive grew faster. We were on our way.

Looking out the window, I didn't see any foliage similar to that of Indiana and Illinois. Growing up around Lake Michigan, I'd been used to seeing water. Not here.

Deceptively, the train appeared to move at a slow pace because I had no sense of the length of the journey. At times it seemed as if we were moving backwards instead of forward. Losing perception of time and travel, my mind began to focus on our unusual experience. We had been invited inside Nancy's personal car—an invitation not extended to any of the other Fulbrights aboard. We had no idea why we had been so privileged.

We couldn't help wondering where our encounter with Nancy would take us. Maybe because she had met many people, similar to us in many ways, during her various travels around the world, she realized that we were only human beings to be treated with dignity and respect, like all the others she had met. How much longer could she continue to shower us with attention and affection?

"I'll order some tea and sandwiches," Nancy announced as the countryside whooshed by my window. "An attendant should be along shortly."

"Forget the tea," I said hungrily, "the sandwiches will be fine, thank you." But Nancy didn't forget the tea; Britishers never do.

Thinking back to around 6 a.m. that morning, when we had gotten off the boat, I hadn't had much to eat at all. I was eating eggs on toast when the announcement of our passing through the channel isles came over the intercom. That's probably all I had eaten all day, passing up the seemingly endless coffee and juice. Vivian preferred not to get up that morning; she said she was seasick. Many passengers were suffering from similar symptoms, but it was most likely mere anxiety than mal-de-mer.

Nancy put us at ease. The three of us sat in a sort of triangle, with Nancy between us, always at the apex. We'd all removed our shoes; they were strewn under the seats around her small tea table, as she called it.

Perhaps because of the time when she was born (1879) or the place where she grew up (Danville, Virginia) or her heritage (British), Nancy Langhorne Astor had great command of the English language. She said that her many tedious, arduous civil responsibilities afforded her ample opportunity to develop and utilize the language. She certainly displayed her considerable verbal abilities that day.

I thanked Nancy again for her kind words on the dock. "I had felt good up until that time," I explained, referring to how the use of my racial identity had negatively affected me. "But you have made me feel like a full-fledged, representative American citizen."

Receiving the Fulbright award and this further reinforcement from Nancy made me feel worthy of representing the United States abroad.

She was glad to hear that I had pride in being black. I told her slavery sought to rob us of our humanity and pride. "The agenda of slavery was to dehumanize us," I said. "We have to develop the sense that we have a chance to be somebody."

As the enchanting conversation swirled, it dawned on me that we were dancing on the train. We were making our own music. Nancy was enjoying herself.

She displayed her immense charm by giving a twirl, in stocking feet, on the cushioned seat next to the aisle, across from us. We were startled at the least but joined hands with her for a brief exhibition of our common dance talents.

Nancy altered her graceful position, evidencing earlier years of artistic talent, and exhibiting flashes of her younger years. Savoring the opportunity to enjoy a new dimension of activity, we joined Nancy in our own rendition. We clapped, heartily hugged, and admired each other's footwork.

It was a spontaneous and immediate emotion, reflecting, in a simple way, the natural social attitude at that very moment. Nancy expressed some form of feeling of the American Negro in her dance. The movements were more along the lines of jazz rhythm, and Nancy enjoyed that.

She was an extraordinary woman; she once danced with Kings and Queens, Princes and Princesses—now she was dancing with the McCrays, strangers from Indiana, alone and in her private car.

Chapter 3:

On Board with Lady Astor

The glow of newfound friendship was settling upon us. You could tell that Nancy didn't like being bored, and we proved a lively pair for her.

Nancy was not shy, not in the least. Her hugs and kisses were plentiful. We felt as if we had known her all of our lives.

What I could not understand, though, was why Nancy had selected me, a black American, one out of a hundred Fulbright students, to share our histories while enjoying the privilege of traveling in her compartment.

She had been caring and loving towards people around the world for so long, so often, that the two of us felt as though we were just two more drops in the bucket. Maybe she realized that no matter how many people she'd seen, or parties she'd attended, no matter how much royal fanfare she'd enjoyed, we were still human beings to be treated with dignity and respect. Perhaps she understood the gravity of the color of my skin, distinguishing me from the rest of the Fulbrights.

Was her past challenging her in the present, I wondered. She was very aware of the intense racial turmoil boiling in America at that time. She had been traveling back and forth across the Atlantic for much of her life, as far back as the turn of the 20th century. Being raised in the American south and then ending up in England with a seat in the House of Commons, then also having the opportunity to travel around the world and see how the issue of culture and race was perceived globally, she must have been very concerned with America's obsession with distinguishing identity by skin color.

Nancy had to overcome racial stereotypes and the prejudice she came by "naturally" as a girl growing up in the post-Civil War south—her own and other whites' attitudes toward her house servants, themselves descended from slave families. She could not understand the situation and circumstances in which she was born and reared. It was now so unreal and unbelievable. The time was ripe for

Nancy to evaluate her past. She was a victim of circumstances.

She praised racial progress at home, in terms of
sports (Jackie Robinson entering Major League Baseball)
and entertainment (Sidney Poitier starring in *The Defiant
Ones.*) She might also had been thinking about the laws in
Virginia forbidding black and white interaction in such
situations as riding in the same train car together.

Nancy had seen pictures and films of Lena Horne,
the black movie actress of the '30s and '40s, but she was so
beautiful that most whites didn't consider her in the same
discussion as other Negroes.

"Lena Horne and Harry Belafonte were mainstays
at the Waldorf Astoria," Nancy enthused. "The big
American stars make the circuit here in London and in
Europe."

*   *   *

Nancy appeared contentedly relaxed and at ease
and it became contagious within the train car. The feeling
was like getting rid of a heavy winter coat at the first signs
of Spring.

After some time in Nancy's private car, we became
just as relaxed. We felt comfortable with each other's

personalities; we felt as if we had discovered a long-lost relative. She was appreciative of this palpable connection, implying that our southern heritage was also part of hers. Nancy was not uncomfortable with how immediately our discussion had turned personal (in fact, she had encouraged it), nor was she discomfited by body contact; touching, holding hands and embracing were common means of communication for her, too, along with laughter mixed with seriousness.

"Where are you from?" I asked Nancy, hesitantly.

"I was born in Virginia," she glowed, "just north of the North Carolina border in a town you've never heard of, called Danville." She grinned, happily showing pride for her home state.

"We later moved north to Charlottesville. I'm one of five girls; all very close and happy. Oh yes, we had two brothers, but we dominated them. It was a girl's life!"

Nancy's family meant a great deal to her, and each member was unique in some way. Her sister Irene was known back in America as the "Gibson Girl" for her outstanding beauty during the 1920's. Though part of a wealthy family, Nancy admitted that she grew up not knowing what being wealthy entailed. She learned later on the responsibility to help those less privileged.

"You were not far from my home," Vivian chimed in, "only a few miles up the mountain to Asheville, North Carolina."

Vivian was often reluctant to discuss her wonderful home state. When pushed, she talked unending about the Biltmore Estate, which was, at one time, the largest house ever built in the new world, and was within minutes of her home. Negroes are tightly knit in her hometown of Asheville. From the days of slavery, segregation divided black and white and placed a palpable burden upon the community.

Vivian told Nancy how she attended segregated schools in Asheville. Integration was not a factor in her life—teachers, the church and the community made up an integral part of her family life.

Blacks knew their place in a white community and did little to agitate the white establishment. Education was the main fact of freedom. I was expected to go to college, although a segregated one. Integration was a gradual process, and I did not have to compete in white society until my time at Indiana University.

*   *   *

Our train ride continued and the conversation drifted capriciously.

"What is your religion?" Nancy shoved at us like a boulder. I didn't know how to respond. I couldn't remember the last time someone had asked me my religion.

Nancy's questioning could be a bit exasperating, and we felt cross-examined at times, but I realized people were going to ask me all kinds of questions until I got back home and that I must be prepared with a good answer.

Vivian mentioned that most recently we were confirmed Episcopal but our background was basically Baptist. Nancy smiled broadly, acceptingly, in a manner that indicated she understood.

I was reluctant to ask Nancy what religion she ascribed to, but she volunteered that she was a Christian Scientist. I told her that I was acquainted with the Christian Science movement and that two of my aunts on my father's side were strong participants in the movement, attending the summer conferences in Chicago each year. They were active participants with exceptionally strong faith.

Nancy recalled that she became involved in the Christian Science movement while visiting back home in Virginia but that she did not grow up with the faith. In times of need she drew strength from her faith. Her husband had died seven years before, and she was still undergoing a period of great adjustment. She did a lot of reading and writing in the Christian Science manner and read aloud to any who were available and wanted to listen. The solace she drew from her faith after her husband's death was her main source of emotional strength.

Nancy believed that she had been the recipient of many healings due to her belief. She did not elaborate, but I could see it in her eyes when she spoke of it and pointed to her exceptional health as evidence of the power of her faith.

Nancy read to us a scripture that she had underlined from one of Mary Baker Eddy's writings that she had particularly loved and wanted us to remember: "…Remember that the world is wide; that there are a thousand million different human wills, opinions, ambitions, tastes and loves; that each person has a different history, constitution, culture, character, from all the rest; that human life is the work, the play, the ceaseless action and reaction upon each of these different atoms."

Back home, my cousin Odessa, who also subscribed to Christian Science, strongly believed that her faith was healing her blindness after she had lost her vision. Before her blindness, she wrote page after page the week that she was visiting in Chicago, reading and underlining words and scriptures taught during her sessions. It was obvious from my discussions with her that much learning, believing, and understanding had taken place.

All Odessa talked about was Mary Frances Baker, a leader in the Christian Science movement. I commented that she must be a great woman, not knowing her at that time.

Listening to my cousin and conversing with her, I could tell she believed very strongly in her spiritual experiences. The more she wrote and read, sometimes aloud, the greater the perceived experience.

Odessa's religion did not involve singing hymns, although I know she liked Negro spirituals. Hers (and Nancy's) religion was more writing and remembering.

People of all racial and ethnic backgrounds attended services with her.

"I believed she relied totally on her spiritual beliefs of Christian Science," I said to Nancy. "She strongly believed in Mary Baker's teachings."

*   *   *

Nancy saw us from the inside out—warmly welcoming us. Perhaps it was her faith that allowed her to accept us even before she met us.

Nancy's concern now was relieving those internal ailments that had been afflicting her. The strength of her religion had allowed her to focus on those things most important to her, rather than social needs and the concerns of her earlier life. She was now beginning to see herself from within.

Nancy was not visualizing some earlier version of her self—when she was in unofficial beauty competitions with her sisters or when she became accepted in the world of high society. Now, instead, she was accepting and strengthening the values that she acquired through her Christian Science faith.

*   *   *

"You are coming to England at a good time," Nancy remarked. "The United States will be defending the America's Cup. It is the most prestigious and famous sport in sailing. The race will take place around the Isle of Wight, where you will be living. Americans aren't aware of this sport, but the boys and girls in your class will know every facet of it."

"It is called the America's Cup because America was the first to win it. America has had the cup for over a hundred years," she giggled, showing no partisanship.

I kidded Nancy about her dual citizenship, but I knew her heart was somewhere down in Virginia.

Nancy said the race would be monitored by colored lights in front of the Royal Yacht Club, not far from where we would be staying. A green light would indicate whether the U.S. Columbia was ahead; a red light meant the British Sceptre had the lead.

*   *   *

When I asked Nancy if there were any particular Negro people that she held in high esteem, she said Marian Anderson was her number-one choice. Marian was an amazingly talented singer who was once turned away from an all-white music school in the early 20's but persevered.

She performed in London in 1930 and then toured Europe, from Italy to Scandinavia. When she returned to the States, she battled against prejudice and reluctantly became a prominent figure in the early Civil Rights movement. By 1939, she performed on the steps of the Lincoln Memorial. Though she was regarded for her mastery of Bach and Handel and Tchaikovsky, she sang spirituals like "Gospel Train" and "My Soul is Anchored in the Lord" at the Lincoln Memorial, for an audience of 75,000 citizens. Nancy said she had heard Marian sing in both London and the United States. She said she knew that one day we would get the respect and dignity that any American could expect. Racism was the worst of American problems.

Nancy communicated well—through gestures as well as words. Her hands, feet, and face were constantly in motion. It fascinated me. Her hands floated and bobbed in the air like kites.

Nancy had so much to talk to us about that I didn't have time to communicate the extent of our enthusiasm and share the excitement of our new adventure with her. But Vivian and I hadn't had time to internalize (let alone analyze) our nearly four days at sea and the various experiences with other Fulbright scholars.

*   *   *

Nancy was an inspiring person. She encouraged us in a manner that stimulated our imaginations. She was forthcoming, even when we asked her questions of a perhaps more personal nature that might require self-examination, such as, "What was your life like in the House of Commons, as the first woman to be seated?"

We knew a question like that would take away some of the uneasiness of our own weary minds.

"Women weren't designed for those kinds of jobs," Nancy responded. "I was not welcome at first, but I stood my ground and fought for the rights of people who thought they didn't have any. Some of the members were initially infuriated, but I won them over in time." Nancy's face emanated confidence. "Some of those war years were glum and bitter, and we sacrificed tremendously for the freedom we are now enjoying."

"What are you doing with yourself now that you are not participating in government?" Vivian asked her in a soft voice, apprehensive to pry into her personal business. "I suspect that you are probably still involved in an abundance of activities that keep you busier than your schedule allows."

Nancy replied, "I'm letting many things go and seeing as much of my family as possible since my husband's passing. I do take excursions back and forth to the U.S. and visit Virginia occasionally."

It was during one of her travels from America that she had met and later married Waldorf Astor. During their marriage, Waldorf, a successful and prominent member of Parliament, was succeeded in the House of Commons by his wife.

"The home place in Danville is not the same, nor is the community," she continued, "Now and then, I visit the 'big house' north of here. It is called Cliveden and I want you to visit there on one of your holidays." She paused. "It has been my main place of enjoyment over the last thirty or forty years."

"We'd love to visit there," Vivian replied, relishing the thought. "It sounds like one of the English castles that we read about but never thought we'd have the opportunity to see or visit."

As we later discovered, it was a castle, of sorts, but actually more of a vast, three-storied house, built in the classic Italian style in the 17th century as a retreat for the Duke of Sutherland and surrounded by numerous breath-taking gardens. The Astor family obtained it before the turn of the 20th century, and it became a place for prominent characters in politics and the arts to gather socially, for strolls through the gardens or for the occasional fox-hunts.

*   *   *

With immeasurable casualness, she used her private telephone line to arrange for us to meet Prince Charles, as his birthday was approaching. "Prince Charles will celebrate his 10th birthday on the 14th of November and you will surely want to be at his school for this occasion."

Vivian and I acknowledged that we had much to learn about British history and that attending the celebration could only advance our cultural cognizance of our own history in the United States.

"Charles is now 'His Royal Highness: The Duke of Cornwall', among his many titles," Nancy said, smiling. "I can arrange a visit for you to see His Royal Highness amidst his elite environment sometime in October, prior to his birthday celebration."

Everything to this point was beyond the widest scope of our imagination. This woman, with her kindness and electrifying personality astounded us. We raised our eyebrows and smiled at each other. This was our first year—our first *day*—in England! How long would Nancy remain in our lives and our future plans, we wondered—and hoped.

We didn't have time to think about what was happening to the other Fulbrights. They must have been on another section of the train as we all were expected in London for orientation the next day.

Nancy served us continuously with tea, along with crackers, cheese, and some kind of cookies they called "sweets." We soon got tired of that. Nancy knew, being American-born herself, that this menu would not satisfy us fully.

"There will be no fast-foods and 'Kentucky-Frieds' where you will be teaching," Nancy stood up, both hands on her hips to emphasize her point.

She laughed out loud several times. These weren't just smiles—I could see her teeth, all of them, which seemed to be in good shape and contributed to her friendly grin.

"You will miss hamburgers and hot dogs as you know them in America," she said, adding quickly, "What are your favorite foods back home?" as if she would forget had she not asked at that very moment.

That was not a disinterested question. As an American, she knew exactly what we ate back home; but she had an ulterior motive for asking; she wanted to know our favorites in case she prepared a meal for us during the coming year.

"Cal," she declared, "you and Vivian will get used to English meals here, but not overnight." She knew for a fact that it would take some time. But she was confident we could do it. Nancy knew that making a cultural adjustment in our eating habits would be an important phase of our transition. "After all, learning about foods is a major part of cultural familiarization. I've experienced the whole range of different types of food in many countries and have acquired many good tastes."

My hope was to participate in as many forms of British culture as possible in my year in England. I told Nancy that I had left all of my expectations about culture, including foods, back home. I came here with an open mind.

She then asked, "Vivian, are you a good cook?" She glanced up out of the corner of her eyes, tilting her head, as if she were afraid to look Vivian directly in the face when asking such an astounding question.

Showing again that she displayed outstanding humor, she said, "Vivian, you don't look like you came here to England to do any 'real' cooking."

Vivian grinned and said, "I didn't come to England to cook. In fact, I didn't bring any cooking utensils or even a fork. I look forward to learning about the culture of the people here and to share my culture with them," she emphasized in a voice louder than she had at any time on the train.

"You will have to shop each day and prepare your own foods on an individual basis," Nancy informed us. "Ice boxes as you know them don't exist here in Hampshire. You probably will have an area in your home that's called a 'cooler' that will keep out the heat but not the cold. Mind you, there is no such thing as cold here! Wait until you try our beer."

She grinned with unbounded joy.

"Don't kid me now, Nancy" I exclaimed with a definite certainty. "Who ever heard of warm beer?"

I was now beginning to exert my feelings after about one hour into the excursion, which already seemed like half the day with Nancy. Not that she was a bore—it was merely the overwhelming nature of her personality. Her pronouncements about food, for example, had quite oppressed us—even though we knew the information she imparted was to our utmost advantage.

Nancy was aware of the wide range of cultural foods available in a country as diverse as America; however, she also knew that, back home in Virginia, the dietary choices for the Negroes in her inherited family had been limited, the selections minimal.

"Let's have some more refreshments," Nancy insisted as she flashed her beautiful smile.

"No more tea, Nancy," I squirmed.

"You'll get used to tea instead of your regular coffee. Try pouring your milk and tea together. Teachers drink cups of tea every day. Let this be your first lesson," Nancy happily demonstrated. "You adjust the amount of the milk but pour them together." Her repeated demonstration showed perfect coordination. "You too, will be just as good in a few days."

"You'll get along fine here in England."

What did Nancy mean when she told us that? Many things rushed through our minds—was she referring to our looks as Black Americans, or maybe our grammar, or the way we dressed, or the values we shared with the rest of the English-speaking world?

No doubt she considered her own southern upbringing in Virginia, learning about the many cultures and sub-cultures unique to America, and thus knew that we would experience no more difficulties than any of the other teachers coming to Britain. For, at various times, Nancy reminded us that, although she was first and foremost an American; her southern culture crossed many lines and even conflicted with her English culture at times.

"You'll get along fine here in England."

Apparently Nancy felt we passed the test. Vivian and I exchanged glances in hopefully positive agreement.

A brief, comfortable silence fell over the three of us, filled by the rhythmic clicking and rocking of the train along the tracks.

"Other than your English dictionary," Nancy said, "I would suggest that you get a map of the British Isles and familiarize yourself with the country. In fact, my first gift to you will be a map of Hampshire County. It will also include an accumulation of the things you need to know about the Isle of Wight."

"Also," she continued, "I want you to have my special book of English idioms that I have used many times."

"I know a few idioms that I've learned from some English students at Indiana," I said nodding, reflecting back to my college days as a Hoosier.

Nancy was able to make us get in our comfort zone of being just ordinary people. She was ruffling up our feathers, you might say, externally and internally as well.

*   *   *

That announcement made over the loudspeaker— that "an American Black" was to teach in the British Isles—still bothered me. I wondered about how the students I was going to teach would accept me…would my skin color be a factor in our relationship? I didn't want to be seen as a 'black teacher,' though I am proud to be black, but I didn't know how to accept the situation.

Nancy knew that I was not a black coming to Britain but a colored person from America, not under-standing his place in a complex world.

She was the kind of person one would be delighted to know intimately. The strangely high amount of comfort we felt around her made it more than understandable to desire a soft squeeze or a hug. Looking at us with those glowing eyes, she recognized the feeling and reciprocated.

I could tell she was ready for a new adventure in her life—she knew that she had lived it to the extreme and that now was the time to taper off and enjoy some new aspects of American culture.

She thought it was great to have some personal time, numerous hours in which to reflect intimately with us. This opportunity hadn't presented itself in this manner before in her life. It was an awakening.

It would be after I returned home to the United States that I read more in-depth about Nancy's family problems and her life in general. It probably was for the best that Vivian and I did not really know about Nancy until after arriving in England.

She revealed to us that she was able to forgive many of the sins of the world through her strong inner-beliefs.

Since her retirement, she had been enduring a unique transition. She had no one to depend on and no one depended on her. The McCrays fit exclusively into her life—just perfectly, at least for the moment. We were the next stage of her life and probably the last one.

She asked me what life was like, growing up on the south side of Chicago. With Nancy nearing the end of her life's journey and me only beginning one of many adventures, I started to recall my own family history—and how it had come to define who I was up to this very moment, sitting in Nancy's private car.

Part Two:

A Sharing of History

The Irving Gay Family. *Front*: Mamie Patterson, Ella Gay, Essie Mae McCray. *Back*: Augustus Gay, Talmadge Gay, Daisy Morrow, Irving Gay Jr., Fred Gay, Robert L. Gay, Sr. (not in photo)

The McCray Family. *Front:* James Charles, Essie Mae. *Back:* Marjorie, (James) Calvin, and Bernard.

Chapter 4:

McCray Family History

The colored people on the South Side of Chicago, in Woodlawn, sought education as a means of advancing themselves socially and economically.

McCray family home on 69th Street

Most of our neighbors back in Chicago were teachers and postal workers with a sprinkling of lawyers and doctors. Single-parent families were unheard of then, and most homes were of good quality.

At the time of our arrival in England, the world was changing, becoming more complex as the Civil Rights movement back in America was gaining more and more momentum. I was beginning to feel very optimistic, then, about the future of America, because I felt that integration was becoming a possibility in America.

My own family had moved north from Georgia—first to Hartford, Connecticut, around the end of World War I, and then to Chicago in 1920.

I was born at St. Luke's Hospital, just south of downtown Chicago. Newly arrived blacks from the south had just recently started using the hospital. There was one black physician there, Dr. Daniel Hale Williams, who would later gain great fame after performing the first successful heart operation.

My family, church, and community challenged me. Most students in my class had educational objectives that included college—even though my counselor did not see the value, in the mid-1930s, that a college education could provide for Negroes. There were few role models and even fewer realizable occupational choices.

These would be, however, the years of Chicago's own Black Renaissance with the rise of writers like Richard Wright and the buzz of Chicago's jazz scene.

My mother related to the Renaissance as a period of happy times for blacks in the arts, in music, literature, and politics. A period in which blacks enjoyed togetherness not equaled before. All of her children were born during this period, after World War I and into the Great Depression.

I did not think that I came from a disadvantaged background. After all, I did have my family together and a host of concerned relatives who cared about each other. I was fortunate to think that I might one day go to college.

*   *   *

During the summers, we walked to the Lake Michigan beach at 67th Street. A fence divided the blacks and whites at 71st Street.

There was little money during the Depression, but a little went a long way. A three-cent trolley ride could take you downtown to the "loop," where you could visit Carson-Pirie Scott & Co., the only air-conditioned store in Chicago in those days.

On Sundays, we went to Berean Baptist Church, on 52nd Street, just off State Street. We rode the street car during those days, as there were no other means of affordable transportation for most people. The automobile was becoming popular, but the Depression had financially drained the country.

In 1936, dad received his WWI bonus and bought a 1936 Chevrolet; it was like a toy for the whole family. Few people in our neighborhood owned an automobile; we were proud. Dad had a hard time learning to shift the gears and crank the engine. Gasoline was 13 gallons for a dollar.

My sister Marjorie was the oldest of three children in our family. I was next, and my brother Bernard was the youngest. Our growing up was rather orderly; our daily lives were routine. We ate dinner together as a family every day except when dad was away on one of his long trips west to Los Angeles as a Pullman Porter. He usually sat at the head of the table, my mother at his left and Grandma Gay on his right. The three of us children sat at the other end.

Our home was a two-storied square brick building uniquely built in the middle of the block with a large yard. We had more space to play than most kids on the block. Mom was a self-made horticulturalist; she planted and maintained all types of plants and flowers.

Dad always reminded me to take the "extra step" in any job or opportunity, that, as colored people, we had to be better than our competitors. In school, if "extra credits" were available, we would be encouraged to earn them.

The colored people on our block in Woodlawn sought realistic goals for their children, but poverty and lack of opportunity hindered many African Americans in

Chicago. Most blacks lived on a subsistence-type income. These people whom we knew and grew up with determined our behavior. We all knew right from wrong. Neighbors felt a cooperative obligation to reprimand a child whose behavior seemed promiscuous or insulting.

My high-school academic program consisted of four years of math, science, English, and Latin. Most students today don't get that much, particularly the requirement of Latin.

I'm not really sure why I took Latin—all I remember is that I had a great teacher, Muriel Allen, my favorite teacher, and she insisted each year that I take Latin again the next year. She was an excellent teacher and she made me see something in Cicero's orations; she made me feel a part of them.

I never enjoyed my English literature class because the teacher didn't even come close to making me feel as though I were a person of the British Isles.

The way she read it, Alfred Lord Tennyson's poetry did not have much appeal to me. If I had known that one day I would be teaching in England, near Tennyson's home on the Isle of Wight, reading his poetry to my students, I might have put more effort into my English literature class. I thought it boring at the time.

It is a teacher's responsibility to bring the subject to life, to communicate it in terms the students can not only understand but feel. In senior year, there were only five students in the Latin class: me, my friend Thomas, the Friedman twins, and a girl whose name I can't recall. We studied together many times, and I learned a great deal about good study habits.

Mrs. Allen had no personal bias and wanted me to enjoy a subject that held little appeal to other students. She didn't emphasize grades; she merely urged me to do the best that I could in the subject. She had me feeling like a successful gladiator competing in Greek and Roman sports. Why else would I take Latin for four years? I am sure she probably saw some opportunity for future educational development and knowledge for me, but there was a sense of mystery in her teaching. After four years, she knew me as no other teacher had before—she understood.

Looking back, I wonder how much better off the whole class of whites would have been if they had also been taught meaningful Negro literature and history.

Those students might have developed different perspectives for their future lives.

I don't recall the American Negro being mentioned in any aspect of the curriculum during my days at Parker High School. I learned about African heritage at home, in my community.

There was plenty of diversity at Parker, but not of the black and white variety. Being the first black at Parker, I had no "separate but equal" curriculum. I believed that I had the same intellectual opportunity as all the other students.

Just as I was on the ship headed to England, I was the only black in my English literature class, and I felt that greater emphasis on the Harlem Renaissance, or the history of slavery would have brought us together in closer camaraderie.

While talking to Nancy, I had remembered that all of my high school teachers had been white—my relationship with other races and cultures had been positive all my life. Later on in life, I realized the gravity of the benefits of my experience—deceptively hidden as they were at the time: I was able both to learn and teach in environments where the people's cultural background differed from my own.

It's true I was one of only a few blacks at Parker High School, but it was closer to my home, on the south side of Chicago. Most students in my neighborhood went to other schools, as boundary lines dictated high school districts. Black families had not yet moved to our area of the south side of Chicago.

The meaning of freedom was not the same for me as it was for my parents; each sought freedom in their own special ways.

"My parents strongly believed," I told Nancy, "that educational opportunities were the most important aspects of freedom. During the Depression years and later, my mother, Essie, became involved in politics and the right to vote became another aspect of freedom."

After his participation in World War I, which he infrequently mentioned, my father, Charles, was disillusioned by segregation and lack of job opportunities for Negroes at home. Now that Negroes felt a certain amount of freedom since slavery, they felt a need to get involved in local politics and church activities.

I was proud of my dad, who worked as a Pullman Porter. The Pullman Palace Car Company manufactured railroad cars designed to accommodate sleeping. Through the first half of the 20th century, the company hired African Americans to be porters; at one time the company was the largest employer of African Americans.

"Several members of my family were Pullman Porters," I said. "When they got together, they shared stories about people who rode the trains." These people, I gathered from their conversations, were the exception, rather than the rule, and were of a higher socio-economic status. Anyone who rode the Pullman cars was more than likely first-class.

I was unaware of the toll that the job took upon my father. In my later years in high school, he said to me, "Whatever you do, don't be a Pullman Porter."

I remember going with dad in 1941, my junior year in high school, to the office of A. Phillip Randolph, in downtown Chicago, to support his effort for a march on Washington. This effort would help Executive Order 8802, providing equal employment in defense industries.

At the time, I didn't understand the political implications of my father's involvement with Mr. Randolph.

We, my family, seemed first class, at least in our own eyes, as we didn't know what privileged people did other than have more money. Their only luxuries seemed to be their exclusive ability to ride first class on the Super Chief from Chicago to Los Angeles.

In those days, all kinds of trains were traveling to and from Chicago—the Santa Fe, the Chief, and the Super Chief. These were looked upon as glamorous transports for the privileged. I knew that one day, after getting an education, *I* would ride one of the Chiefs to California.

*   *   *

During and after the Depression, my mother became involved in politics, and the right to vote became another aspect of freedom. Political and economic powers were neighborhood discussions.

My parents, although not complacent about the direction and movement of Negro Americans, realized great improvement in their own lives as Americans and had great hope for their children in the future.

The opportunity to vote for the first time was a joyous and momentous occasion and an opportunity that had not been available to them before to express self-pride.

My mother became a precinct captain and supported Congressman William Dawson on the south side of Chicago. He was a personal friend of hers and probably the most powerful black man in Chicago at that time.

I remember her switching political parties from Democrat to Republican. It was not a matter of which party freed the slaves but rather the present condition of society at the time that was most important to my mother.

*   *   *

As a family, we enjoyed making the best of life's difficulties, as they were then. We thought that we got the most out of the life that was available and that there were many people less advantaged than us. The Great Depression of the '30's brought many families closer together.

Dad, in particular, kept us abreast of the current segregation laws affecting eating, transportation, and other public activities that would generally affect our personal everyday living.

The plight of many blacks who moved from the south looking for better opportunities was unbelievable. They left the paternalistic, casual racism of the south only to encounter the sometimes more virulent, often disguised racism of the north.

*   *   *

Nancy had now had some time, albeit a few minutes, to compare her own memories of growing up in Virginia. Those memories of her youth were probably what caused her to travel continually back and forth across the Atlantic from New York to England.

But now her thoughts were preoccupied by the unusual circumstance of sharing her private care with two black Americans whom she had never met before.

Nancy's relationship with the Negro during her early lifetime was of a close, familial kind, she told us. The exchange of education and culture was an exchange of values that were understood and appreciated. She recalled, begrudgingly, how African-American men were treated as boys, socially and literally—though I knew she saw me in a man's role, similar to that of white men in Western culture.

"My family moved to Chicago in the '20's," I said. "I was born in 1924. There was much racial tension in the city at that time. My grandmother was a white woman who married a black man and raised a family. She bought a house; we moved in, and that caused a big disturbance. All of her children and grandchildren had to fight, not quite literally, these people who harassed her on a daily basis."

During the 1920's and '30's, Negroes moved to the very south of Woodlawn between Cottage Grove and St. Lawrence, ending at 69th street (upon which my family lived). Negroes did not venture to cross that street, where the Pennsylvania Railroad dissected the neighborhood.

"I knew what time it was every day when the Broadway Limited passed," I said. "It took 17 minutes from the Union Station in downtown Chicago, and it was always on time."

There were a few whites in the surrounding areas during that period, but they moved out fast during the Great Depression years of the early 1930's.

We were fortunate to have neighbors that would be classified as middle and upper class, even by today's standards. Things were based on class even among the aspiring blacks.

Growing up in Chicago, I was able to maintain balance between the white and black world without difficulty. My parents helped to mentally prepare me for integration. It proved to be an advantage later on as I climbed the educational ladder.

"Looking back at the values that my parents taught me, I would be hesitant to suggest that they should have done it any differently," I told Nancy. "They supported our efforts to do the best we could in school."

Going to Parker High School during the day and returning to my home community, I was able to participate in my family's and my neighborhood's culture. My friends may have kidded me a bit for attending an all-white school, but they never rejected me. Most of us were busy anyway, as my close friends participated in sports or extracurricular activities.

"It seems," Nancy said, "you were able to live comfortably on both sides of the fence."

"Yes," I said, "I didn't see myself as a different person living in two environments but rather as having an educational and social advantage."

On a trip to Washington D.C., Nancy had visited Dunbar High School, an all-black school and said she saw excellent educational experiences there. She knew that, if properly taught, a racially diverse student body would substantially improve our perspective in history.

Nancy revealed that, when she visited Negro audiences during visits to the United States, she made many unsuccessful attempts to sing "Lift Ev'ry Voice," the Negro national anthem, which was immensely popular in the black community. She admitted that she needed assistance in reaching some of the notes. She didn't find it unusual that the black community had its own national anthem. Nancy was not impatient as she listened to me talk about race. She understood race more deeply than I.

In my senior year, I read two books for Oral Reports, and I will never be able to forget either: *Green Dolphin Street* by Elizabeth Goudge and *Studs Lonigan* by James T. Farrell.

Both books were on the senior reading list and recommended because our teachers thought we could relate them to current events in our lives. I was glad to be able to read both novels, even though my senior year was crammed with a part-time job and playing two sports, which took up most of my time.

Both books dealt with personal and dramatic issues and presented life-threatening situations in ways that were understandable to a high-school senior, in terms that a high-school senior could relate to.

Green Dolphin Street is the story about two sisters and the man they love, who grow up before the reader's eyes over a 40-year period. It is fiction that reads like reality. It takes us around the globe—from England to New Zealand—and introduces us to different cultures and societies (like the Maori), different world situations and points of view. Like *Studs Lonigan*, the book came to life through class presentation and discussion.

I was moved by the tragic death of teenage Studs. "Studs lived and died on the south side of Chicago, in walking distance from my house," I told Nancy. "People did a lot of walking then, even though a street car ride cost only three cents. We, my friends and I, and sometimes my family, walked two to three miles to the library on 63rd Street, near the University of Chicago."

I paused for a moment and reflected more on my hometown, then decided to declare to Nancy, "Being born in Chicago, one needs not worry about going anyplace else. Chicago has it all."

Although Chicago was second to none, I usually met my friends in "The Loop," which was the heart of the city. The Loop is where the elevated trains meet and branch out over the city.

Talking to Nancy about it, I felt myself trans-ported back to those glorious days of my youth, striding underneath the noisy metal snake of the Loop. Seeing it then, on the train, so vividly in my memory, I thought to myself, "This is my hometown. This is where I was born. My culture is here on the south side of Chicago."

In those days, the late 1940's, I rode the streetcar downtown just to see some of the new inventions that the city was implementing: escalators and elevators and air conditioning. It was a thrill: we didn't have television or fast food, but the things that they did have were fantastic.

*   *   *

The journey to Champaign-Urbana for my freshman year in 1942 was not easy. Most Negroes that I knew who came to the University of Illinois knew how to cope with the double standards—they had the backbone to adjust.

Eating and living on campus was unrealistic at that time. Learning how to live, to adjust to a learning environment so different from your culture was in many cases disconcerting. Education meant surviving a system.

*   *   *

When I arrived to teach in Gary, Indiana in 1952, I was aware of the great steel town with a diverse population and a school system known around the world: the Gary (Indiana) Plan.

The Gary Plan offered several educational programs in each school, utilizing various time elements of the day and night, in conjunction with community and business organizations, to educate all ages. Many cities saw the educational and economic advantage of this type of curriculum.

Pulaski School where I taught and into which my interchange counterpart Cyril Doughty would be assigned was situated in a predominantly black neighborhood. The Gary, Indiana, schools were integrated, but Cyril would be teaching only black students. Race was not an element of required information in the Fulbright process.

Chapter 5:

World War II

In my senior year, on the morning of December 8, 1941, that my classmates and I—clueless about the events in the greater world—stumbled into speech class. I was prepared to give my speech on Lincoln's Gettysburg Address when the teacher, Mr. Bloom, interrupted me.

"I had spent weeks learning to memorize it," I said. "But then Mr. Bloom told us, 'The Japanese have bombed Pearl Harbor,' in a very solemn voice."

Most students were stunned, not knowing how to react. For most of us males, it meant signing up for the draft.

I enlisted after my first semester at the University of Illinois.

My mind was made up to apply to the Coast Guard after learning about the exciting life aboard a ship as a sailor, to live at sea. It was my second choice after the air force. I had initially applied as a candidate for the Tuskegee Airmen, but the application process was lengthy and time consuming; a war was going on in Europe and Japan, hence my application needed to be accelerated.

Nancy praised the relationship between the British Commonwealth and the United States, and their gallant participation in both wars.

"What did you do in the Coast Guard during World War II?" Nancy asked, surprised that I wanted to talk about it. This was one of the few opportunities I had to discuss the Coast Guard, as no one had ever really asked me until this moment.

"The Coast Guard was a segregated unit," I said, "as were other branches of the service during the War. I went from Chicago to New York and spent my first month in a room waiting for a collective group of Negroes to form a unit for 'boot' training. Many of us studied together, learning about navigation, meteorology, Morse Code all in a few short weeks, which required diligent learning skills and the proper attitude."

"During that month," I continued, "I was stationed in a high-rise building in the financial district of New York.

The address was 14 New Chambers Street. I was on one of the top floors. I was assigned to a Negro sailor with several red stripes on his left sleeve and a white shield on his right sleeve, just above the wrist."

I paused and watched Nancy take another sip of tea, losing count of how many cups we'd shared at this point.

"This was my first day with the Coast Guard. 'Stand up straight!' came the shouted order. 'My name is Alex

Alex Haley

Haley,' the sailor said, 'I have been in the Coast Guard for several years and you will be assigned to me until the number of recruits to fill a unit is complete. Until that time this room will be your home. These stripes indicate that I am a Petty Officer, second class, the lower stripes refer to the number of years I have been in the Coast Guard."

This Alex Haley and the man who authored the famous novel and chronicle of the tribulations of Negro slaves, *Roots*, were one and the same. He told me he had enlisted as a Mess Attendant, third class, for the Coast Guard in 1939, since "messboys" were the only Navy ratings permitted to Negroes at that time. The soon-to-be-famous writer would eventually become chief journalist in the Coast Guard in the mid-1940's.

I mentioned to Nancy that I was proud to have been in the U.S. Coast Guard during WWII. My early training in "boot camp" was in a segregated unit, all colored. This was a surprise to me, at first, but not terribly shocking. Our unit received twice the amount of physical training as white units, mainly to keep us occupied. Of course, we therefore excelled in all of the physical maneuvers.

After completing my basic training, I arranged for and got a meeting with Jack Dempsey, the former heavy-weight champion of the world, who also happened to be a base commander. I asked him if I could participate in his athletic training program, which consisted of physical training of new 'boots' at the Manhattan Beach Coast Guard Training Station in Brooklyn. Dempsey was overjoyed that I had sought him out as he had needed another physical instructor. I wasn't hesitant to tell him that one of my goals was to one day teach physical education. He graciously accepted me as a member of his training staff.

"He never asked me if the recruits I'd be working with would be white and I never asked him," I said to Nancy. "I don't think it bothered him one iota, and it certainly didn't bother me. Later I found out that Dempsey had recruited some other Negroes, all of whom had some college background—notably, Eulace Peacock, a former Olympian; Herbert Thompson, a multi-year National Champion in indoor track; Homer Gillis from New York University; and me, a freshman from the University of Illinois. We won Penn Relay events in the quarter mile relay against other military and university organizations."

Dempsey asked me one day if I would be interested in attending a service school as well as continuing in the athletic program. I was hesitant to positively commit myself to a "yes" answer. Jack said, "There are four schools; you can make your selection and let me know."

Jack did not realize that, under ordinary circumstances, I would not be allowed to enroll in either of the two classes that I selected. I selected Quartermaster School and Jack promptly enrolled me. I am sure that there were many objections in class because of my race.

It was difficult being in Quartermaster School and managing to teach "phys-ed" part-time. Moreover, I realized that I would be the first colored in an all-white unit, training for a position of authority above deck. "Most Negroes had jobs requiring less skill," I told Nancy.

"Not only was I the first Negro to integrate the group," I continued, "but I was the lead person in all of our drills and marches. Of course, the Coast Guard was a strictly segregated service and, if Commander Dempsey had not personally enrolled me, I would not have had the opportunity to attend a service school. I took that in stride, too."

"What was life like at sea?" asked Nancy, recalling all of the journeys she had made across the Atlantic Ocean between England and the United States in the years before Lindberg's flight, when crossing the ocean by boat travel was the only means of travel.

"My Coast Guard vessel," I began, "was named Madalan." In peace time, it patrolled the East Coast of the U.S. During the war, it was used as an anti-submarine vessel. I was one of three quartermasters.

U. S. Coast Guard cutter, "Madalan"

"John M. Timken was the skipper of the Madalan. His family owned the Timken Roller Bearing Works in Canton, Ohio. He was a graduate of Harvard University and the Harvard Business School. His family's business was known for providing roller bearings not just for some of Ford Motor Company's earlier models but for supplying companies worldwide. We traveled from Guantanamo Bay, Cuba, to Halifax, Nova Scotia."

I told Nancy that German U-boats threatened our supply lines to England by sinking "liberty ships" off the eastern shores of the United States during 1944. They were called "liberty ships" because, like everyone and everything, they were doing their part for the war effort.

Returning to the University of Illinois after WWII, during the summer of 1946, I signed up for the flying class in the University's School of Aeronautics and received my pilot's license.

Over the years, I continued to fly as a hobby and an opportunity to continue my professional relationship with the university.

$$* \qquad * \qquad *$$

There was absolutely no way for Vivian and me to understand the heroics Nancy was involved with during World War I and II, as a member of Parliament.

"Those were perilous days," Nancy emphasized. "Both World War I and II were horrible, and I'm sure that I won't live through another one. We suffered dearly through those years."

As a member of the House of Commons, she took matters such as these very seriously and very personally. She knew of the contributions of black soldiers arriving in England during 1943 and the cooperative effort made to win the war. She stated that she met many of the WAC's (Women's Army Corps) who were black. They worked in the first-aid units as nurses.

Feeling so close to Nancy now, it was hard to imagine how bitterly adversarial our countries once were in the late 18th century.

I reminded Nancy, with a gleam of good humor, grabbing her hand and squeezing it, "The United States declared war on Britain in 1812, didn't we?"

Nancy's smile showed that she could take good humor as well as dish it out. We both got a big grin out of that.

The Civil War, a few decades later on from then, was an even greater war (one of the bloodiest in human history) and, in a way, is still being fought on many contemporary stages, dividing America in many ways.

The mood grew somber again as I reminded Nancy of this unfortunate fact.

"It took the Fulbright Program to get you here," she exclaimed loudly, putting her arms around the two of us. We were now "the three musketeers"—one for all and all for one.

Chapter 6:

Diversity and Civil Rights

When we think of diversity, the first thing that hits us is skin color. When other cultures think about diversity, they are not as heavily fixated on the race issue as we are in America.

Diversity is a much bigger issue than race or ethnicity. It's culture. It's religion. It's a way of looking at the world and where you came from.

From early times, man, seeking power, has dominated his own kind—not based on the color of the other's skin or his religion or culture (though these were frequently the excuses used) but because of his overwhelming desire to achieve superiority, regardless of the cost.

Throughout my life, I noticed that Negroes got caught up not only in the racial issue of black and white, but also had to contend with the shades of blackness forced upon them by white people. There was a tendency by whites to divide blackness into preferential levels for economic and social reasons. The lighter the skin—the more preferential. They saw lighter skinned Negroes as more like themselves and in general more acceptable in their personal relationships.

We knew that there were few places where we could speak openly about race—the way we were with Nancy in her private car. She understood the enormous value of initiating social discussions such as this one.

When she was young, Nancy assumed no equality between the races, but there was no evidence of that early attitude in her manner with the McCrays.

Nancy had no way of realizing that, within a few short years, the Civil Rights movement would be in full swing. Only the American Revolution, in my eyes, equaled the gravity of that historical event.

Nancy said she admired women like Sojourner Truth, who was born into slavery and gave her life fighting for black women's rights and the rights and freedoms of other blacks.

"There are a lot of barriers that have to be broken down in our society," she said. "It will take more than laws to mend the social ills that have been established for so long."

I understood exactly what Nancy meant and knew she was talking from experience. She had realized a long time before that she had a responsibility to give something back. She never forgot that her family was all colors.

Nancy was able to understand the transition to freedom of those Negroes in her close family relationship—something I could not completely understand coming from my environment growing up in Chicago.

"We are a very sensitive race," Vivian said, looking Nancy squarely in the eye.

"I have not been through what you have, Vivian," Nancy admitted, "but I know, from my past experiences, what you mean."

Nancy was as sensitive to race as anyone, maybe more so. She lived with both races concurrently, while she was growing up, when Negro women worked for her family in the United States.

Nancy knew from her own early experiences and her mother's that there were great liabilities in being a woman. She knew Negro women faced even greater barriers.

The idea of a black woman getting an education was not in the forefront of Nancy's thinking when she was growing up; in fact, neither was the idea of a white woman's opportunity—the woman's place, no matter what her skin color, was in the home.

All women, educated or not, could not travel back and forth across the Atlantic at will, as Nancy did. She refused the sexist conditioning of her mother and sought refuge in England. She realized that her attractiveness and economic well-being would offer her greater opportunities to meet men of her status.

Nancy agreed with me on the subject of education for women. She complimented Vivian on her achievement and said she wished she had taken advantage of a college education.

Although Vivian, who was college educated, was different from any black women she had ever associated with on the same personal level, she knew where white women drew the line when it came to race and particularly class.

Growing up, Nancy thought and acted for Negro women who were not taught to think for themselves or act independently.

Nancy knew that Vivian was not in poverty but that her roots were in slavery, as were her own roots.

"I learned early on," said Nancy, "that people will go to great limits to gain various freedoms others took for granted…not only blacks in America but in many places around the world to which I've traveled."

Nancy had seen all the stages of human growth and development in her own life, and she was now willing to share.

Nancy said she understood how society and the government had shaped racial discrimination and social injustice during her early years, growing up in America. She said institutions like the Fulbright Program helped creatively reshape American society. The Fulbright Program, she said, although political and social, could only have a positive effect on the economy and poverty in America.

She said she admired Rosa Parks, a strong woman similar to many she had known and who, three years earlier, had had the audacity to defy segregation laws in Alabama by refusing to give up her seat to a white man. Racial equality and segregation became very heated issues in America after 1955. Nancy said she knew that these issues were larger than her.

I mentioned that I was a great admirer of Jackie Robinson. Breaking the color barrier in baseball was getting to the heart of America's most popular entertainment, our national pastime. His character was a challenge for me, as I had faced discrimination in sports at the University of Illinois, during the '40's, not just on the playing field but in the classroom as well.

Although Nancy had her feelings about Negro women during slavery, they were personal and not to be divulged openly. The societal mores of the period demanded they value slave masters' families above their own.

Those black women close to Nancy while she was growing up were strong, mentally and physically—they had to be to manage two families at the same time. They had inner strength.

I mentioned to Nancy that my mother's father was born right after slavery had been abolished in 1865. "My past is not long out of slavery," I said. I can remember thinking, when my father would remind me how closely connected my grandfather's birth had been to slavery, that it seemed so long ago. "I guess I've come a long way since then."

I described how my dad had fought in a segregated unit in France during World War I—seeming to indicate that black American soldiers weren't fighting to protect the same freedom as whites.

Nancy knew the inequity suffered by Negroes in Virginia was an internal suffering and that her learning the effects of Christian Science proved useful in her ability to understand their internal pain.

Nancy saw this as an opportunity to apologize for the misgivings of slavery in her home state.

Nancy had no way of knowing that in the near future, her beloved home state of Virginia would regret its participation in slavery and would come just short of publicly apologizing.

*   *   *

"The people you meet here," Nancy said, "will have a definite effect on how you direct the rest of your life." She knew of the challenges we would face.

But there she had a charming way of always lightening the mood of the room with her smile and sense of humor—which was unique. She snickered about having color designations for bathrooms: "We don't have separate facilities for men and women…or for people of different colors on this train," she said.

Nancy explained that Britain was a country of many races and a multi-cultural society. "The problems of multi-cultural Britain are in many ways similar to those in the United States," she said.

* * *

Nancy knew I was a mixed-race offspring from two or three generations back, the product of more than one family.

"You are a McCray, aren't you?" she asked jokingly, but directing the conversation with her wisdom. "You have blood from part of the British Isles."

Her thinking and knowledge was, of course, deeper than mine. In my younger days, we children didn't discuss our family heritage, and we didn't ask too many questions.

But, when we got older, we overheard our elders speak, sometimes seriously but sometimes jokingly, of our blended heritage.

Grandma Gay, as we called her, who lived with my mother and me until the age of 100, had twelve children who were all different skin colors. These relatives played an intimate part in my cultural understanding.

It was difficult, however, to get any significant history of my parents' true blood relatives. We were descendants of blacks, whites, and Cherokee Indians. I was never able to tell how much black, white, or Indian was in me, an American, having all the rights and privileges as those paying homage to the Statue of Liberty upon returning from abroad.

I became fascinated with science, heredity, genetics, and reproduction in my college days. I became particularly interested in "the pea theory," which was a nickname for an experiment of Gregor Mendel in the 19th century. He studied a "blending theory" of heredity, that both parents contributed the inherited traits of the offspring, like the mixing of paints. Peas were a primary test subject of his experiments. I was a pea in a multi-racial pod.

*   *   *

During my lifetime, I have celebrated many Supreme Court decisions that had affected the Negro, specifically concerning progress towards social equality, but the one that had the most realizable importance was the 1954 *Brown v. Board of Education* decision. During my beginning years as a teacher, race in the classroom became the hottest issue in America. It was up to my fellow teachers and me—the adults in the school (a microcosm of society)—to sort out the disputes among students.

Nancy applauded Mary McCleod Bethune for creating educational opportunities for black girls and diversifying their experiences in and out of the home.

We spoke of other activists as well, such as John Brown, whose acts of defiance were not as subtle or dignified as Rosa Parks'. His message, however, is admirable; even though he paid for it with his life, he attempted freedom nonetheless.

Nancy felt that she was at that point in her life where she could reflect on all of her experiences with Negroes and share them intimately with the McCrays.

She certainly felt that we upheld the highest of American values and social status. And she had known and interacted with people who possessed a wide range of values and came from all social strata. With all the traveling she'd done, the places she'd visited, the people she'd met, she could probably speak for a representative sample of black life in America.

Given the span of her life and the scope of her travels, Nancy would have seen many changes in social and educational reform, much economic upheaval, and the almost complete social restructuring of minority groups.

In 1949, I was told in my hometown of Chicago that, although I was certified, there were some schools at which I could not teach. That was merely one example of racism.. I said to Nancy, "The discrimination at home is not limited to educational institutions but found at all intersections of American society."

"I know exactly what you're talking about," she said. "But I have seen change in America over the past fifty years, changing the attitudes and beliefs of both black and white, rich and poor."

"The Supreme Court ruled against segregation in public facilities," I granted. "When I visited Vivian six years ago, by train, in her home in North Carolina, I rode in a "separate-but-equal" facility. I was the only one who had a curtain wrapped round him.

"'Separate but equal!'" I huffed, still struck by the terrible indignity. "Draping the curtain didn't mean equal or using the same facilities. It was the matter of respect that counted."

Nancy agreed. We were displaying our affection towards one another—not trying to equalize it. Our differences, however minimal, didn't conflict.

Nancy knew that Homer A. Plessy was arrested for refusing to leave a whites-only passenger car. "They are gradually doing away with that separate-but-equal doctrine," she said, "as evidenced in the Brown vs. Board of Education case."

Traveling was not easy for blacks in the early 1950's.

"When we drove to Vivian's hometown, Asheville, North Carolina, from Chicago, we stopped at Mrs. Adams home in Barbourville, Tennessee, for the night," I related to Nancy. "Motels were not open to blacks at that time. Mrs. Adams had a grocery store with a couple of extra rooms for visitors in the rear of the store, and she rented them to us. We stopped there many times even after the Civil Rights Laws forbade segregation in public places. She became a part of our extended family."

*   *   *

We were fortunate enough to understand and realize Nancy's intentions. She knew more about this phase of our heritage than we did, even though we both grew up learning about black history, mainly from our own families. Black history is broad and deep—two words one could also use to describe Nancy herself. She knew that decisions about people had to be made on an individual basis, not on the basis of race.

*   *   *

Many of my older Kappa Alpha Psi fraternity brothers from my time at the University of Illinois, who lived and worked in Chicago, came to Champaign, Illinois, to give us support during the critical times of segregation before and after World War II. Outstanding Chicagoans like Earl B. Dickerson, prominent insurance executive; Robert E. Lewis, educator; Earl L. Neal Sr., attorney; C. Roger Wilson, business executive; J. Ernest Wilkens Sr., professor at the University of Chicago; Thomas B. Mayo Sr.; and many others were among those who came.

During the early '50's, Negro teachers in the southern states were traveling to northern schools to get advanced degrees because segregation laws at that time prevented blacks from attending white universities. And, while they could matriculate there, they couldn't *masticate*. Vivian and I could not eat on the campus at Indiana University. Segregation was at its height. President Wells, a close friend, allowed us to eat with him in his personal office.

At the University of Illinois, black students found eating establishments on campus unwilling to serve them, and off-campus eating was even more discouraging. At the Steak & Shake on Green Street, black students could only purchase hamburgers at the back door. Living accommodations on campus were non-existent.

Nancy knew of the privilege she enjoyed growing up in the south, where there an abundance of Negroes, recently free from slavery.

The comparisons were incomprehensible—rich and poor, black and white, one educated and the other (the blacks) prevented from learning by law.

Nancy had seen firsthand what it was like to be born black and not have privileges.

*   *   *

"The British know more about America than you think," Nancy explained assuredly. "They want to learn more, and they want to see and hear it from you."

She almost shouted and made a fist to pound the arm of her chair. "Cal, you have hit upon several people that I would like to know about myself, such as the doctor who performed the first open-heart surgery. Our conversation today has been great!"

"The association between our two countries is remarkable," I said, "they are like family—not always agreeing but understanding the relationship."

Chapter 7:

The Fulbright Program

Nancy and I both saw the Fulbright Program as an opportunity to explore other cultures as well as to learn more about our own personalities and talents.

Being a Fulbright was a great experience and opened up a world of possibilities that were otherwise not available for Negroes at that time.

In the mid 1950's, going abroad was unimaginable for most Americans, especially black Americans. For blacks, getting stabilized in America after slavery was their only realizable dream. The idea of teaching abroad and sharing my ideas of my hometown and my home country with other segments of the world seemed like something accomplished only by presidents and secretaries of state.

J. William Fulbright must have realized that people all around the world would be brought into closer proximity through educational exchange. He joined the Foreign Affairs Committee, as a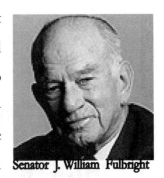

Senator J. William Fulbright

Representative and encouraged the United States to participate in what would become the United Nations. He became a Senator in 1944 and created the Fulbright Educational Program in 1946, dedicated to the goal of mutual understanding through international relations and educational advancement.

The program is the largest U.S. international exchange program. It provides students, scholars, and professionals opportunities to pursue international graduate study, advanced research, and teaching (university, elementary and secondary schools).

Now entering its 62nd year, it has awarded more than 250,000 scholarships around the world.

To be a Fulbright Alumni means realizing the vitality of mutual understanding between the people of the United States and the people of the world.

In 1976, its 30th anniversary, in the name of honoring the camaraderie and tradition of the Fulbright Program, as well as acknowledging the invaluable inter-continental connections it had established, alumni convened the Fulbright Association; an opportunity for a global alumni movement for rededication to the main tenet of the program, namely, mutual understanding among peoples of the world. (fulbrightalumni.org.)

Years after our return, in 1993, the J. William Fulbright Prize for International Understanding was established. Recent recipients include President Bill Clinton, General Colin Powell, President Jimmy Carter, U.N. Secretary General Kofi Annan, and Nelson Mandela, the first democratically elected President of South Africa.

"You two don't know the impact that this Fulbright Program will have on your lives at home and abroad," Nancy had said to me, aboard the train.

Many years later, I found out that my State Senator from Michigan, Jackie Vaughn III, had been a Fulbright Scholar to Oxford—that made me proud, considering the positive effect his efforts had had upon the Detroit community. He undoubtedly was one of the first Blacks to receive a Fulbright award, and he preceded me to the British Isles.

"The value of your meeting people on an individual basis is what the Fulbright Program is all about," Nancy emphasized. "Your relationship with cultures abroad will drastically improve your understanding of diversity in the United States."

Nancy recognized the intrinsic value of the Fulbright Program. "The relationships you two are developing are powerful. Your being the only black tells me something…" Nancy leaned, her eyes expressive as she gave Vivian one more hug. Vivian was awed by Nancy's sincerity.

Part Three:

Nancy's Challenge; Teaching in England

Tower Bridge, London

TEACH IN EUROPE - J. Calvin McCray and his wife Vivian, both teachers at Pulaski school in Gary, sailed Aug. 8 from New York to teach in the United Kingdom during the coming school year. They will teach under the educational exchange program of the Department of State. Arrangements were completed by the office of education in the Department of Health, Education and Welfare.

Chapter 8:

Nancy's Plans

Being with the McCrays today, she thought, was a bright spot in her life. She said it was difficult to recall a more meaningful and memorable sharing of her intimate life.

Nancy seemed so freewheeling, as though she was not worried about tomorrow. Maybe she didn't care if tomorrow ever came…? *I will dance more, take off my stockings, do more hugging, laugh louder and shed a few tears*, she may have thought.

We knew little about places to venture in England. Nancy had used her on-board telephone to arrange for some speaking sessions at various English Speaking Union Organizations that I knew nothing about. I warmly accepted the challenge.

Apparently, that wasn't the only thing Nancy had used her on-board telephone for. She had a challenge for Vivian, too.

*   *   *

Nancy was quite the persuader, though she didn't claim to be such as savvy as her close friend, Winston Churchill, Britain's Prime Minister during WWII, whose stirring oratory helped rally the country and see it through its darkest hour.

Nancy, supposedly, once told Winston, "If you were my husband, I'd put poison in your tea."

Winston replied, "If you were my wife, I'd drink it."

Regaling us with that particular anecdote, she chuckled, "As you know, Winston had an American mother, just like me."

*   *   *

In the back of her mind, Nancy had plans, plans for us, plans that she thought could be accomplished.

Nancy's long life was marked by many accomplishments—most of them successful, but some not so pleasant. She had some regret for many of the things that happened in her past. Nothing could be done about yesterday, but she could do something about today. We didn't realize it at the time, but Vivian figured heavily into these plans.

The rhythmic clicking of the wheels on the tracks filled a brief silence. Nancy was stretched out, resting on some pillows, when suddenly, she stood up and took a breath.

"You must teach, Vivian," Nancy suggested. "The children on the Isle of Wight will love you!" She was very demonstrative, throwing her hands into the air, waving with enthusiasm.

Vivian was speechless and later revealed to me that she had felt a bit imposed upon but at the same time was gratified by Nancy's persuasive encouragement.

Nancy recognized that our backgrounds were a source of richness and would be an advantage in our teaching in England.

"You won't have to do much to persuade me about teaching," Vivian politely responded while looking directly into Nancy's eyes. "I was accepted to teach next year with the Fulbright program but refused the opportunity so that I could accompany Cal this year and explore the program's benefits as a tourist and housewife."

Vivian rose and lightly hugged Nancy around the shoulders. "I am now a teacher on leave of absence. I am not allowed to accept employment under conditions of Cal's grant; I can only travel as a family member."

Nancy, more determined than ever, showing every bit of authority left in her now seemingly smaller body, demanded that Vivian agree to teach.

"This is an exceptional opportunity to get involved in the culture of the community here. You will enjoy the people and particularly the children. You *will* teach, won't you?" Nancy asked, her voice tinged with a plea. "You may be the only black person that some of the children will have seen or have been involved with—certainly in the capacity of teacher."

At first, Vivian did not enthusiastically accept Nancy's plans for her to teach, as she had not prepared herself mentally for such a task during the past school year.

She was reluctant to commit herself fully, not knowing the consequences. It was important to know what grade levels and subject matter she would teach. The thought of not knowing who she would teach temporarily boggled her mind.

Vivian knew that an all-white class would be interesting and the exchange of culture would be a challenge. "They might ask me why my skin is brown and not white like theirs," she said tensely. "Or they might want to feel my hair and wonder why it doesn't feel like theirs. We might not find any common ground."

"You would communicate well with the students in the island," Nancy assured Vivian. "Your English is fine. Your vocabulary is extensive, and you use many words that students will not understand immediately. However, just be patient and share your culture with them. We do not purport to be masters of the English language here, but the majority of the people speak English at various levels of competency. In addition, this opportunity would be another step of your educational and cultural journey.

"Your life experiences are varied, and your goals and aspirations are unlimited," she reasoned, with characteristic warmth and charm.

"Your future is ahead of you," she said, "and your past is just as complicated as mine. I had to get out of the country and search for a new beginning. Your past is a vehicle for preparing you for the future."

A moment of silence settled between us, filled by the rhythmic clicking of the tracks outside. Nancy could tell her persuasions were working on us, but, of course, I'm sure she never had a doubt that we would resist.

*   *   *

It appeared that Nancy was examining our family's decision making. Would a black woman make a decision as important as who works or not?

Nancy knew that, back home in Virginia, her mother—as a woman—had limited opportunities. The most she could aspire to was supervising the home—mainly bringing up the family and managing the servants. Nancy imagined that she would have done the same if she hadn't taken her own life under control.

"Cal, how do you feel about Vivian teaching?" Nancy asked, looking first at one of us and then the other. Did Nancy think that I had anything to do with Vivian's decision to teach? Or did she believe that Vivian made her own decisions?

Vivian had never been in an encounter where there were such determined expectations of her. She squirmed in her chair, as if what I said would make a difference.

Vivian was challenged, and I wanted her to make her own decision, to teach or to enjoy the life she had planned in her mind this past year. Nancy was definite and persistent: "You will teach, won't you, Vivian?"

I reminded Vivian that we could still do the things we had planned together, but her responsibilities as a teacher would be time consuming and would require the kind of lesson planning she did back home in Indiana.

It was like making a million decisions in a few minutes. Vivian had only one choice—yes or no. The only good, reasonable choice was to say, "Nancy, I will teach."

With a subtle smile, Nancy leaned in and hugged her.

In saying yes, Vivian was floating at a higher level, somewhere around the ceiling within Nancy's stateroom. It took several minutes to adjust to those stressful moments, not knowing how to respond.

This was a dream come true. The magnitude of her obligation and the length of time it might take to realize what Nancy had thrust upon her had not yet occurred to Vivian. Nancy was going to take care of all that, anyway.

"Your status as an accompanying spouse of a Fulbright Scholar will be changed to non-resident employee effective tomorrow, August 14th," Nancy announced admiringly to Vivian. "Effective in two weeks, you will get a salary based on your education and teaching experience. There are legal papers you will need to sign as well, and I will make the arrangements to obtain a labor permit for you to work in Britain."

Nancy was reading Vivian's mind; as though she knew all along that her answer would be positive.

"Just think," Vivian said, "two days ago I was a housewife, and today I am a paid teacher in the United Kingdom. I will still fulfill the objectives of the Fulbright teacher as an American teacher abroad."

Nancy pursued Vivian's teaching assignment with determination and effectiveness unseen in our level of society back home. Her persistence was a bit over-whelming to Vivian. What grade level would I teach? *Why did Nancy do this to me?* she wondered. It was too late now; she had given Nancy the final "yes," and in a few days the Education Committee would meet with Vivian in London to validate her teaching assignment.

Nancy saw the challenge she put to Vivian as her responsibility—a chance to bestow upon another woman, a black woman, boundless opportunity and the prospect of an extraordinary experience. Although Vivian was excited about the responsibility, the initial shock was difficult to withstand.

Nancy recognized, in our dual opportunity to teach, the rewarding vitality of exposing English children to the African American experience. Bringing our culture into English classrooms would illustrate the great social sea change that had occurred less than a hundred years ago for blacks, from slavery to freedom to education: two intellectual, culturally proficient and capable teachers that personified the triumph of the Civil Rights movement, here as American representatives of the concepts of the Fulbright Program abroad.

Nancy saw this as her opportunity to advance this discourse on race, in her own way. She felt a wonderful quality of freedom; she knew that she had lived her life well, and this fateful meeting with the McCrays was another way of celebrating. Her mental strength and character were indelible; she had the positive manner of making one feel at the top of their capacity.

We sat back in Nancy's comfortable seats, lounging for a moment and analyzing all of her planned events, realizing that we could only absorb so much in one day.

*   *   *

After the excitement of Vivian's decision subsided slightly, Nancy, once again, became more conversational.

"Things are different here—for example, food and terms for food—but the students will help you adjust," Nancy cooed. "Don't expect things to be Chicago-style or to have French fries as you know them; no, indeed, they're called chips here. Forget about sloppy Joes."

Hee, as before, when she'd gone on a similar tirade aboard the train, we thought Nancy's humor was outrageous, but we enjoyed it anyway.

"It'll be fun being British," Vivian chimed in.

"What are your interests outside of education?" Nancy asked after a sip of tea, hoping to get onto something less sensitive.

"My life has been full of sports, all kinds, but, since I've been married, I have narrowed down to golf. You probably know that takes up many hours, but it is satisfying and challenging. I have brought my clubs with me in case the opportunity arises for a few rounds."

Nancy's smile curled slowly, "I will arrange for you to get in a few rounds after you and Vivian settle in. "I appreciated her offer and gracefully accepted. "England is known for its history of golf and its courses, you know," she beamed, as she displayed her golf grip and demonstrated a back swing, which I admired.

"My real interest is horseback riding," Nancy said and lost herself for a moment in fond memories of riding. "You don't believe me, do you?" she asked with a sincere smile. Now, somewhat distracted in her attempt to convince us about her achievements and showmanship in riding, she strode back and forth from one end of her compartment to the other, still in stocking feet, obviously comfortable in our presence after volunteering so much personal information to us.

Then—mercurial as always—she was off on another topic.

*   *   *

"You will undoubtedly get homesick, but the two of you can manage together,' Nancy said, adding that she felt the weather would be a main factor in adjustment. "It doesn't get as cold in Hampshire as it does in Chicago or Gary, Indiana," she said, "I've been to Chicago, and I well know its characteristic winds."

Not missing a beat, she continued: "You will find the Red Funnel Steamer an exciting and unique method of transportation from the island to Southampton. On board, you can relax and enjoy a new form of transportation unlike any you might find at home."

"Vivian," she said, looking her in the eye, "you will now need to shop, specifically for clothing to wear in the classroom. The temperature will not be as warm as your American classrooms." She paused to show a grin.

British school buildings did not maintain the high temperatures that we were accustomed to in the United States. Sixty-eight degrees Fahrenheit was considered normal in the Isle of Wight (but—after we experienced it—Vivian thought it was colder than that).

"You will find the shopping wonderful in Southampton as you travel back and forth to the Isle of Wight. They have the same stores as they do in London, but not as many."

With shopping plans covered, Nancy moved to address finding the right hair-stylist for Vivian, referring her to Madame C.J. Walker, whom I'd heard of but whose personal history I didn't know much about.

Vivian mentioned that she knew of Walker's hair-development methods for conditioning the hair of black women. Nancy saw the revolutionary concept as a means of raising the level of acceptability of the black woman in society.

Nancy had her mind set as to what she wanted to plan for the McCrays. Although bold and direct (and *directing*), she was open-minded to the most excellent possibilities and choices imaginable. It was like tasting all the chocolates. She was the first of many warm and friendly people we met during our stay—though none was quite *so* warm and friendly (*and* overwhelming) as Nancy Astor.

Later on that night at the Strand Palace Hotel, Vivian smiled happily and said "Cal, there is no way that I could have said 'no' to Nancy."

We were infatuated with Nancy's charm and encouragement. She liked us for who we were, and it did not matter that we were colored people. In fact, it may have been one of the real reasons that we were now in Nancy's possession. From the very beginning, there was no escaping Nancy's web.

The British Committee for the Interchange of Teachers

between the United Kingdom and the United States of America

Nancy, Lady Astor

requests the pleasure of your company

at a Reception to be held at

Dartmouth House, 37 Charles Street

Berkeley Square, London W.1

on Thursday 14th August, 1958

from 3 to 5 p.m.

Tea

Invitation from Lady Astor

Chapter 9:

Orientation

Since we hadn't traveled in the same train compartment with the others, I knew that Orientation would be the last time we would see the rest of the Fulbrights, as they would be scattered around various parts of the British Isles—Ireland, Scotland, Wales, Liverpool, and Birmingham, among others.

"Have you had an opportunity to read the Orientation materials for tomorrow?" Nancy asked.

"No, we haven't," Vivian responded with a shy grin. "We haven't had time yet. They were given to us in a packet of several dozen pieces of literature five days ago. We were just taking one day at a time."

"I have the invitation here in my bag," I said, "I'll read it aloud: 'The Orientation Program is sponsored by the Honorable Lady Nancy Astor'—need I read more?" I lowered the page.

"Is that you, Nancy?" we both yelled, knowing the answer, then impetuously grabbing and pulling her up out of her reclined position, overwhelming her small frame. For the moment, we were all one. Our ardent affection for Nancy had reached its apex. "We are slowly and helplessly learning who you really are," I said with a smile.

Nancy would preside over the reception the next day at Dartmouth House in London. British Commonwealth representatives and members of the English Speaking Union would be there, along with many other distinguished guests.

*   *   *

Slowly, the train came to a stop with a symphony of clicks from the tracks, groans from the brakes, and eruptions of steam from the engine. We arrived at Waterloo Station in London in the late afternoon, close to evening, but the sun was still up, and it was still hot.

Nancy let us know that we were in her territory of government, although she no longer presided over the territory of Hampshire, since her retirement.

The list of hotels for Fulbrighters to use during the orientation was posted on the S.S. United States. Arrangements had been made for our arrival. From a list of highly impressive hotels, Vivian and I had selected the Strand Palace. Nancy approved of our choice ("in the middle of the rich and romantic era of the City of London," she said).

As we prepared to depart for our lodging, the time came to briefly part from Nancy until the Orientation, and, as she looked at me, there was a glow of pride in her eyes.

Nancy, an American first, knew what psychological and physical struggles that we, as black Americans, had encountered to get an education and to arrive at this point in our lives.

"I'll see you at the Orientation," she said with a smile.

*   *   *

The next day at the Orientation we saw Nancy at a distance in the great hall among seemingly hundreds of people dressed in their finery. The reception hall was breathtakingly large, and I was dizzied by how many people were breezing by us as we entered.

Nancy moved through the crowd, reminiscent of

the day we arrived when she was looking for us on the dock. Nancy held out both hands, greeting us with

Cal, Vivian, and Nancy at Orientation grace and dignity. There were no introductions to be made this time. We were no longer strangers. In fact, it seemed now as though we were very old friends, as if we'd met in Chicago or New York long ago.

Nancy, showing no sign of fatigue from yesterday's

activities on board with the McCrays, moved impatiently around, meeting the other Fulbrighters whom she'd had

Fulbrighters attending orientation

little opportunity to greet the day before.

At the reception, Nancy made sure that we were meeting the "right" people and getting a chance to sample some of the many refreshments displayed around the room.

It appeared that we were a prime target of guests and members of the English Speaking Union. It was probably the largest congregation of educators we had ever seen and they all wanted to meet us.

"Welcome to England!"

"Where are you from in America?"

"I've never heard of Gary, Indiana…"

…were some of the common questions and comments among the dozens of people we met. Hopefully, I remember thinking, they will not ask me anything about Republicans and Democrats.

I was reluctant to get involved in any racial discussion regarding what was going on back in America. President Eisenhower had sent the 101st Airborne Division to escort the "Little Rock Nine" (as they were called) into Central High School in September of 1957, almost a year prior to my arrival in England. Eventually, the 101st ended up staying for the entire school year. The newspapers in London were continuing to cover the situation in Little Rock, Arkansas, where schools were being closed in reaction to the integration of black students.

It didn't matter that we were the only blacks in attendance. We really did feel welcomed. For the moment, we forgot about the fact that Federal troops had been sent in by President Eisenhower to protect Elizabeth Eckford in Arkansas, as she tried to enter another school with white Americans.

Nancy said that she had met President Eisenhower and that he was one of her great generals, along with George Patton. Why was he now fighting another battle— one that was greater than that of World War II?

Now, Eisenhower, twelve years after returning from Europe, had to use American troops to fight for the freedom of all Americans. It was this type of freedom I expected for myself as a war veteran when I hung up my Coast Guard uniform in 1946.

Vivian and I believed Nancy was committed to social equality. She fought for the things she wanted and believed in. She was a warrior. She believed that we should have the same opportunities as she had and that it was an accident that she was white and we were black.

The Little Rock situation was hard to figure out from what I read in the London papers. Their interpretation made me feel happy to be away from home. The Little Rock authorities were about to shut the schools down completely (a decision born from disagreements over integration), and that didn't go over very well in Britain.

Ironic, wasn't it? Back in Arkansas, they were discussing closing all the schools to keep blacks out, and here I was, a black man, about to teach in England. Somehow or other, that concept didn't make sense. The people at home had to explore and realize understanding between themselves before international understanding could be developed.

Senator Fulbright and Governor Fauvus should have gotten together and found a sensible compromise.

I just smiled when colleagues tempted me to share my thoughts one way or another. Many seemed eager to debate it with me.

Nancy agreed that we should talk about the positive things in the world. Was it worth discussing discrimination and segregation? Are they one and the same thing, I wondered, as I read the articles?

Disappointed and somewhat sensitive about the Little Rock situation back home, I was aware that comparable situations had occurred in Mississippi and Alabama. Little Rock was not a surprise or an anomaly but another in a series of hurdles for American internal democracy.

Gary had integrated its school system, both staff and students, after similar difficulties in other cities in Indiana. The early stages of neighborhood integration were hampered by segregated housing patterns, and school integration was in the planning stages.

My colleague, Dr. Faustine Jones Wilson at Pulaski Elementary, kept my exchange-counterpart, Cyril Doughty, abreast of the social interaction in America while the Little Rock desegregation issue unfurled.

Happily, I learned from Dr. Wilson and the school community when I later returned to Gary, Indiana, that my exchange teacher, Cyril Doughty had enjoyed his teaching experience tremendously and had left with a positive image of America.

We eventually became acquainted with Mr. and Mrs. Hatfield and their daughters, along with Mr. and Mrs. Wileman—all close friends of Mr. Doughty. They were our main consultants and friends whom we confided in about food, weather, culture and educational matters. They were our main source of family life while on the Isle of Wight and our relationship remained strong through the years.

*   *   *

As the Orientation began winding down, Nancy found her way over to us, and we settled at a small table, the three of us, thus recreating our arrangement aboard the train. Gary's school system came up once again, and we began discussing, more intently, education.

Nancy knew the histories of Booker T. Washington and William E.B. Dubois quite well, as they were prominent during her younger years in America. She saw them as two of the greatest black leaders of her day: Dubois in his campaign for Black Nationalism and Washington for rallying support for black education.

From all of Nancy's previous discussion on the value of education, I imagined that her thoughts leaned toward better education for Blacks.

"People should have choices," she declared. "The more education one gets, the better the choice. From my own experiences in the past, I have found few Blacks preferring agricultural and food services as a career. The history of slavery—the demanding outdoor labor required for growing and harvesting crops and the physically intensive requirements of food preparation—was an incentive to make other choices requiring education."

Attendees began to take their leave of the Orientation one by one, and our conversations drifted to other topics.

Nancy, her excitement still not subsiding, said, "How lucky you are to be coming to a holiday resort to teach; Queen Victoria had a residence at Osborne House near the school where you will be teaching. Alfred Lord Tennyson also lived on the island. You must spend some time traveling the Isle as a tourist, seeing each village, one at a time. There are no cities as you know them, only villages and towns.

"The Isle is warmer than most of Britain," she continued with a chuckle, "being one of the farthest points south." She explained that the island was one of her favorite spots to sit on "the green" and relax in the sun.

She smiled as she said, "You might want to sit on the green in front of the Royal Yacht Club and get a different view of the S.S. United States as she passes through the Solent," referring to the body of water between the island and the mainland. "It's a wonderful sight."

The night came to a close and we returned to our temporary lodging, a hotel near the Royal Yacht Club.

After a month at the hotel, we moved into a traditional English thatched-roof house, with all the English trimming one would see in art museums. The house was without central heat and a refrigerator, but we managed the winter. We enjoyed the warmth of the "real" log fireplace.

At that time, as Nancy knew well, we were anticipating a group tour of about a week's duration that included Belgium and Paris. This would be our brief vacation before starting the school year.

We looked forward to the Brussels World's Fair as we were only made aware of it during our journey on the S.S. United States.

"Of course," I told Vivian, "we will have to visit the United State's pavilion, if they have one, and see what the main emphasis is that we're trying to share with the rest of the world."

At the fair, we did indeed visit the U.S. pavilion, to find that the emphasis was on foods—all kinds of American foods.

1958 World Expo in Brussels

DEPARTMENT OF STATE
WASHINGTON

September 10, 1958

Dear Mr. McCray:

    Next year will mark the Sesquicentennial Celebration of the birth of President Abraham Lincoln. To celebrate the Lincoln Sesquicentennial Year numerous activities have been planned both here and abroad. The Department would like to enlist your assistance in this regard.

    The United States Information Agency will sponsor many activities at its overseas installations to commemorate the Sesquicentennial. It hopes that American teachers and lecturers in American studies who are abroad on their awards under the Department's International Educational Exchange Program in 1959 will cooperate with American officials overseas by being prepared to talk on the subject of President Lincoln and to participate in programs honoring his contributions to United States and world history. The United States Information Services abroad will be supplied with abundant materials on this subject that will be at the disposal of American grantees abroad. Your contributions to this celebration will emphasize the importance of the Sesquicentennial and will be very much appreciated by the Department and the United States Information Agency.

    I hope you will enjoy your year abroad. If the Department can be of assistance to you at any time, please do not hesitate to let us know.

    Sincerely yours,

    J. Manuel Espinosa, Chief
    Professional Activities Division
    International Educational Exchange Service

Mr. James C. McCray,
    In care of American Embassy,
      London, England.

Letter from Department of State, 1958

Chapter 10:

Teaching in England

One of our pre-teaching excursions took us to the Isle of Wight for sightseeing. Once there, we checked in at the Grantham Hotel, where we encountered two naval officers of a warship from Pakistan. They were staying in the Grantham when we arrived, and we introduced ourselves as new arrivals from the United States.

It wasn't long before they invited us to dinner.

We ate with them frequently, sharing our new experiences with them. This one-on-one connection, the first of many that I would develop during my time in England, reminded me of Nancy's prophetic wisdom regarding the Fulbright Program.

Their ship, a destroyer type, was a WWII donation from the United States. Great Britain provided any and all mechanical assistance needed for their return to Pakistan. It was commissioned the Shah Jahan.

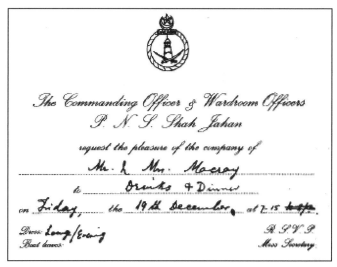

The Pakistani officers chided the waitress, Jill, who was also the hotel proprietor's daughter, for exposing her legs, (a common practice for girls of England and the United States). However, females in Pakistan did not expose their legs. Both officers were headed home to get married, as their mothers had selected their brides-to-be. Our social relationship was extremely cordial, and we enjoyed some of the basic principles behind the Fulbright Program.

Vivian and I were asked to be present at the final ceremony, on December 19, 1958, aboard the ship. Already we were finding ourselves representatives of the United States abroad.

We talked about the foods they enjoyed back home and missed here in England, such as seasoning with curry. A few times they invited us to eat with them when they cooked their own meals while the ship was in dry-dock. We didn't get a chance to reciprocate, though we did come to appreciate their unique and spicy foods. (Twenty years later in Zambia, while I was teaching there, we learned to share in Indian culture as well.)

The conversation alternated from discussions of the zesty taste of the curried beef and chicken to their arranged marriages and brides awaiting them when they returned home. They were a jovial pair, indeed.

The officers wanted to know how, where, and when we met and married. Because of their tradition of marriages arranged by parents, they were fascinated by our different methods of courtship.. Nancy had, days earlier, asked us similar questions but under different circumstances.

*   *   *

We were, indeed, popular residents with almost everyone. Two gentlemen visiting England from Southern Rhodesia (now Zimbabwe) did refuse to eat with us; however, we challenged them to speak.

We got along splendidly with the rest of the hotel clientele—who knew of our connection to Lady Astor and teased us every day by asking us if we had any more "calls from her Lordship." In late September, Nancy did call to see if we had settled in at the Grantham. Jill took the message and informed Nancy that we were adjusting quite well to the climate. We had been out that day, shopping for new wardrobes in Southampton.

The climate was easier to adjust to than the cuisine. As Nancy had warned us, the meals tasted bland compared to the zest and variety of the foods we were used to in America,

Later, Vivian did prepare meals when we moved into the "thatched roof" house closer to the schools. Cooking utensils had been left for us to use—not quite like ours at home, but they did the job.

We bought foods on a daily basis, one meal at a time, as Nancy suggested. We prepared fish and chips, at least twice a week. Invitations to eat out were plentiful.

Parents and teachers were anxious to meet us, and we were happy to make their acquaintances. During the process, I learned to drink the thick lager beer, brewed warm.

I later told Nancy that I would take many British habits back to Indiana with me, including warm beer and fish and chips. (Though, actually, any preference for warm beer was left behind in England.)

On the few weekends when we stayed at the Strand in London, we looked forward to the roast beef served on great silver trolleys with apple pie, their specialty. I asked that my pie be "à la mode." I had to explain it to the waiter. I'm not sure he quite understood.

The first day of school arrived before we knew it.

*   *   *

The students whom I taught

My class, as well as the whole school (children up to age 11) participated in a year-long project, learning about the great migration after the 1803 Louisiana Purchase in the United States. It was the first project of its kind to be taught in the school. They developed a course for the Westward Movement, using hand-made materials to represent all portions of the exhibit.

The American Embassy in London made available books, charts, and pamphlets in American history were made available from the American Embassy in London. Surprisingly—or perhaps not so surprisingly—they gave no information on slavery and Negro participation in the growth and development of America.

I realized though, that ignoring the slave experience would omit the core element to understanding the development of history in America.

I was able to get books and material from the libraries in London that acknowledged the contributions that black Americans made in building the country during that time (the early 19th century).

I learned quite a bit, myself, about American history in that one year: it started with Jamestown, Virginia in 1609 and ended with the gold rush in 1849.

Replica of an old Trysail schooner, similar to those raced in the America's Cup

*   *   *

The students themselves would exude such passion over the sounds of the passing ships outside.

Marian Gladdie, a sprightly student of mine, took ships seriously, as if she owned them. She got a lot of attention by arguing about which ships were bigger.

I'll never forget Stephen Buckell, the captain of our class football team (by which of course, I mean *soccer*), always shouting aloud in class when the S.S. United States passed, blasting its majestic sounds, entering its berth in

Southampton. Stephen knew that he could get a wide grin from me with his exuberance.

Usually it did not loiter in the harbor as it did not have a deep draft, and the tide allowed it to pass. Sometimes ships with deep drafts had to wait overnight until the tide was high enough to navigate. However, if the tide is at ebb, the water is receding, making it impossible to navigate. Larger ships like the Queen Mary, at full draft, looked for full tides to foster easy navigation.

*　　*　　*

Communication with students' parents was limited and for the most part discouraged. Parents were invited to school only on special occasions, such as when the headmistress made appointments to share grading policies with them. When I taught in Gary, I felt it necessary to communicate with parents on a regular basis. Despite my concerns for the development of these Isle of Wight students, parental involvement was not encouraged.

There were 22 students in my classroom, all of them around 10-years-old. My interaction with students, on an individual and group level, was always a warm and endearing experience. I discussed any concerns I had about students, which were always minor, with the headmistress.

During lunch, the students and I compared and contrasted American and British concepts such as money, measurement, foods, and sports. I taught them baseball, and they taught me soccer (their "football"). I was enthused by their eagerness to learn about the American way of life—and this sharing of cultural learning defined, for me, the purpose of the Fulbright Program.

*   *   *

Throughout the year, the Fulbrighters would, on occasional weekends, travel to London for social and educational meetings. We learned to enjoy the British railway to London and look forward to such weekends.

Early in the Spring of 1959, continuing our English assimilation, we ordered an Austin-35, a British vehicle, quite small by American standards, and traveled through France and Spain during Spring break.

We continued to travel in our small Austin for the remainder of the 1959 school year, visiting the small villages and towns. Sometimes, friends of ours would be eager to go with us and point out historical points of interest.

At the end of our venturing, we returned to our home, a humble house called Jerema, on York Avenue in

East Cowes, Isle of Wight. The people in the close-knit community of the Isle of Wight were friendly and always eager to learn more about us as Americans.

*   *   *

I obtained most of my news regarding America on the weekends when we went to London for meetings, conferences, or social events. The local papers primarily covered English events but occasionally covered the world.

I was one of the "local event" covered. I noticed that they had listed me as "a colored teacher arriving in England," which caused me again to wonder at all the different classifications I had been given over the years: Negro, black, colored, and, later on, African American.

During the first week of December 1958, the local papers carried a headline: "Fire in Chicago school, many killed." The details were meager, but the whole world soon learned of the children trapped in Our Lady of Angels School. The fires started just as classes were going to be let out; having no means of escape, 90 pupils and three nuns were killed, and 77 were seriously injured.

As a result of the fire, most schools in the world began the practice of fire drills. I recall the first day we implemented it at the East Cowes Primary School. The students seemed to understand the need for all the safety precautions and exited the building in the designated manner.

Vivian and I enjoyed the intellectual relationship with both the children in our classes and the school community. We welcomed the knowledge, understanding, and compassion exemplified in the Fulbright Program.

$*$ $*$ $*$

Invitation to meet Her Majesty Queen Elizabeth

It was an unusually warm, sunny day in July, 1959 in London, England and we were moments away from meeting the Queen Mother. We were to be greeted by Her Majesty, something she did annually for American Fulbright Teachers coming to teach in Britain.

We mingled in groups, pairing off, saying hello's to those we had met during educational meetings aboard the S.S. United States, meeting others for the first time. We shook hands and smiled as we prepared to meet the Queen mother—a once-in-a-lifetime experience.

Everyone wanted to make a good appearance. Ladies had their hats in place and white gloves pulled on properly at elbow length, and were practicing their curtsies.

Among the crowd I recognized a young man who was not a part of our American family. He was chatting with two ladies with whom I was not acquainted.

Vivian and I strolled over and introduced ourselves as the McCrays from Indiana. The two ladies said they were from Canada and Southern Rhodesia. Eyeing me and extending his hand he said, "I'm from Guyana, British Guyana. My name is Braithwaite, E.R., pronounced *Braffit*."

Prior to our meeting, we both recognized each other as having African heritage. Later we talked about what names we were each called back home.

"Being a part of the Commonwealth, I am black," Braithwaite said.

"Back home in Indiana or Illinois, I am a Negro or Colored, depending on the circumstances," I replied, both of us grinning widely in acceptance. We were both shades of black and both had amazing heritages.

Braithwaite promised to visit us on the Isle of Wight, and I agreed to visit his school on the East side of London.

The next year, Braithwaite wrote a book about his experiences in that East London secondary school. *To Sir, With Love* later became a film starring Sidney Poitier.

After the Queen Mother met with all of the Fulbrighters, Nancy arranged for Vivian and me to meet with her privately the next day, July 7, 1959, for a luncheon meeting in St. James's Palace, near Westminster.

St. James Palace

Vivian, the Queen Mother, and I were alone under the watchful eyes of a palace guard, decked out in his traditional dress and standing at attention during the whole meal. All formal customs and eating formalities were removed at the request of the Queen Mother.

During our meeting, the Queen Mother received a phone call from her daughter, the Queen, who was visiting Chicago that same month to commemorate the opening of the St. Lawrence Seaway, which made Chicago one of the great seaports of the world. She wanted to give her mother an update on her visit to the city.

A guard had approached the table carrying the phone and had set it down by the Queen Mother's plate. We both sat quietly as she spoke with her daughter.

"I have, in my company for lunch, two American teachers in the Fulbright program, who happen to be from Chicago," we heard her inform her daughter. Then, after a moment, she turned away from the phone and said that her daughter would like to speak with me.

I was amazed to suddenly have the opportunity to speak with the Queen, at any time—let alone in such surreal circumstances when she was in my hometown and I in hers—breaking bread with her mother, no less.

We spoke of the Chicago weather, how Vivian and I were doing so far in England with the Fulbright program and how we'd been able to secure a luncheon with her mother. Then the Queen asked if it would be alright for her to call my mother in Chicago.

Again, I was overwhelmed.

A few days later I called my mother in Chicago and asked her if she had received any interesting phone calls lately. Yes, she informed me, she'd spent an hour on the phone with someone who said she was the Queen, but it hadn't quite registered with her—not knowing the history of the Queen or the British monarchy.

"You were talking to the Queen of England!" I half-shouted exuberantly. She then admitted her slight embarrassment at not realizing it at the time. Similarly, Vivian and I had not realized the extent of Nancy's historic influence until we had gotten to the orientation.

That certainly was a highlight of our trip; we wouldn't have met the Queen Mother or spoken with her daughter if it hadn't been for meeting Nancy. We were very fortunate—the opportunity to have lunch with the Queen Mother was an unlikely occurrence for any of my fellow Fulbrighters.

The Queen Mary

Chapter 11:

Homeward Bound

We had seen the Queen Mary several times during the 1958-1959 school year, parked out in the English Channel where we could almost touch her. She waited overnight sometimes for the tide to rise so she could enter her terminal; much of her tonnage was under water, so it was necessary for nature to assist in keeping her afloat.

Although the Queen Mary took a day longer to cross the Atlantic than the S. S. United States, we didn't mind, for we were not in that big a hurry to get back home. For some reason, we felt that we could relax more and enjoy the happy people coming to America who shared the decks and dining halls with us on our return journey. Some were coming for the first time, and others, like Vivian and me, were returning from various points in Europe. It was a rejuvenating jaunt back home filled with more parties, celebrations, Captain's dinners, and fancy balls.

Vivian won first place in an onboard clothing-design fashion show contest for outfits made of materials found aboard the ship. From cigarette cartons, I made a two-foot-long hat depicting a ship, and she modeled it to the tune of "Show Boat," which the ship's band played.

Vivian participating in fashion show onboard the Queen Mary

Pictures of our group relaxing and having fun onboard the Queen Mary

When we returned, we stayed in touch with the Buntings, our acquaintances from our first journey on our way to England. We later visited them several times. They owned a dairy farm in Old Harbour, not far from Kingston in Jamaica. It was there that I learned how to milk a cow. For a native Chicagoan, that wasn't bad.

Looking back some fifty years ago, on the great liners of the past—the S.S. United States and the HMS Queen Mary—Vivian and I realize that those were times of another generation. Both ships were built under wartime specifications and had tremendous capabilities for speed—they were truly landmark achievements of the greatest generation.

Commercial airflight was in their infancy then but quickly doomed those fine vessels. Still, the fantastic memories remain. Our greatest memory was of Nancy greeting and welcoming us upon our first steps into England. That memory led me to writing this book.

*   *   *

Through much of the school year, I learned a lot about ships around the world and what kind of cargo they carried. My students compared the ships by size, tonnage, noise, country, and other factors.

It was wonderful to know that a United States liner broke the speed record for crossing the Atlantic that the Queen Mary had held previously. My students didn't like that, but it helped bring us closer together. They adjusted well after the America's Cup victory of the Columbia over the Sceptre around the Isle of Wight. That was an exciting time to be in the British Isles.

Our students persuaded Vivian and me to take the Queen Mary back to the United States. It was a change in two significant ways. One, we were returning home after a year of happy exchange, full of adventure and new friendships. Two, we realized the many benefits of cultural exchange.

In New York, as I stepped off the gangplank onto the welcoming area and noticed the masses of people—boys and girls, men and women—I wondered what the people might have been thinking. Would any of them have wanted to make the trip that Vivian and I had made?

Maybe not, but I felt quite lucky. Maybe I was one in a million.

EPILOGUE

After returning home to Gary, Indiana, it was difficult to settle down, relax, and savor the worldly experience of the past year. The incentive to explore the world of cultures continued as we climbed the educational ladder and found that learning is endless.

Later on, I spent many years as a member of another Fulbright program, The International Visitors Council of Metropolitan Detroit, providing opportunities for Americans to share their cultural experiences with visitors from abroad. Currently I sit on the board of this association. The IVC of Detroit welcomes international visitors who are sponsored by the U.S. Department of State and has been operating since 1972. (Visit us at http://www.ivcdetroit.org.)

Fifteen years after saying goodbye to Nancy, in June 1974, we returned to the Isle of Wight to see our students and friends with whom we'd maintained contact through the years; they now had children whom we had watched grow up through our correspondence. Some of the students, both Vivian's and mine, had moved to the mainland, probably for better job opportunities; others had married or moved elsewhere.

We toured the island in a car that we rented in London and visited some of the areas that were not on the agenda fifteen years prior. This time, our daughter (who was 15-years-old and had been conceived during that first trip) was with us. She learned about our early travels and some of our cultural discoveries.

We visited the house we had lived in and met the present occupants, who served us several cups of tea, something we hadn't had since we left the island. It was served in the traditional manner which Nancy had explained to us on the train.

Through the years, we learned even more about Nancy. We scanned various media, particularly books. Nancy, when we had met her, was in the last chapter of her life's story. We were glad to have known Nancy when we did because she was an accumulation of all the previous chapters. All that was left for us to do was to summarize. We had met our match in the indomitable Nancy; we had developed a warm affection for her.

Years later, Vivian and I would drink tea on special occasions, birthdays and holidays, remembering Nancy's train compartment and her showing us how to make tea the English way. For some reason, it never tasted the way Nancy prepared it that day aboard the train.

We are forever realizing the effect of Nancy Astor's impressive personality and her encouragement for all to seek another level of human relationships. She was the center of attraction. Throughout our time in England, we were continually asked questions about our relationship with Nancy Astor and how we got personally involved with the first female member of Parliament and one of the most powerful women of her day.

Nancy lived and explored both worlds, black and white, but—when we were with her—we were not sharing our lives as black or white but as human beings. The relationship between Nancy and the McCrays was a human one and not one of color. We appreciated the fact that she felt comfortable with our culture. We assured Nancy that nothing would live more indelibly in our memories than our years of knowing her. We met her during the ebb tide of her life.

Nancy died in 1964 and was buried in England. Her roots were in America.

Acknowledgements:

First, I would like to thank my loving parents, Essie Mae and James Charles McCray, who instilled in me from the beginning the necessity of hard work, sacrifice and maintaining a positive attitude about achieving my goals and objectives. They exemplified the moral and spiritual values that helped shape the path of my life. They believed in me and supported all of my efforts to get as good an education as possible.

Thanks to the many people along the way before Nancy who contributed to my successes; you have facilitated my journey toward helping countless students as a teacher and professor.

During the last ten years, I gathered all of my materials on England and the Fulbright Program. I decided not to throw them away and to write about Nancy. The positive effect that she had, particularly on my wife, was what made me become a writer of non-fiction.

Getting started and committing to a regular schedule was one of the most difficult self-assignments that I had ever undertaken. Once started, though, I worked on a consistent basis, making writing a high priority in my retired life.

I owe a special debt of gratitude to Dr. Virginia Lewis in St. Petersburg, Florida, a former principal at Wendell Phillips High School in Chicago, who wanted to know more about Nancy each year when Vivian and I visited her. Finally, she and her friend Juanita Gonzalez agreed to edit any produced manuscript, compelling me to finish; I am extremely grateful to them. I am grateful to Cassandra Sprattling, who encouraged me through her readings and many suggestions. Special thanks to Jeff Milosevich, a young and promising journalist, for all his help—above all, he was a good listener and thinker. Thank you to Angela Cooley from Kissimmee, Florida, who typed and asked pertinent questions about things I hadn't thought about. Thanks also to Nora Holt, Dr. Melvin Hollowell, Talesha Jester, Venna Winters, and Anne Kabel.

Finally, I would like to thank my wife, Vivian, who shared and endured this dream trip and kept every clipping, receipt, poster, bulletin, handout, picture, postcard, railroad ticket, menu and letter from 1958 and 1959. Without her help, this book and my desire to write it would never have come to fruition. There were so many other things I could write about.

Bibliography

Abrahams, Roger D., and Rudolph C. Troike, editors, *Language and Cultural Diversity in American Education.* Englewood Cliffs, New Jersey. 1972.

Bennett, Lerone, Jr., *The Shaping of Black America.* Johnson Publishing Company, Inc. 1975.

Bennett, William J. *America: The Last Best Hope.* Thomas Nelson (www. ThomasNelson.com): 2007.

Boyle, Kevin, *Arc of Justice.* Henry Holt and Company, New York, 2004.

Braithwaite, E.R., *To Sir with Love.* New York, N.Y. 1959.

Café, William H., *A History of Our Time.* New York, N.Y. Oxford University.1983, 1987, 1991, 1999.

Du Bois, W.E Burghart, *Dusk of Dawn.* New York, N.Y. 1968.

Franklin, John Hope, *Mirror to America*. Farrar, Straus and Giroux: New York, 2005.

Halperin, John *Eminent Georgians: The Lives of King George V, Elizabeth Bowen, St. John Philby, and Lady Astor*. Palgrave Macmillan: 1997.

Hampden-Turner, Trompenaars, *Riding the Waves of Culture*. McGraw Hill: New York, 1998.

Johnson, John H., *Succeeding Against the Odds*. New York, N.Y.1989.

Jones, Faustine Childress, *The Changing Mood in America*. Howard University Press and the Institute for the Study of Educational Policy: Washington, D.C. 1977.

Lewis, Virginia F., Short *Stories from a Long Career*. Third World Press: Chicago. 2004.

Loewen, James, *Sundown Towns: A Hidden Dimension of American Racism*. New Press: 2005

Marlowe, Derek, *Nancy Astor.* New York, 1982

Obama, Barack, *Dreams from My Father: A Story of Race and Inheritance.* Crown: 2007.

Proctor, Samuel D., *The Substance of Things Hoped For.* New York, 1995.

Rowan, Carl T., *Just Between Us Blacks.* New York, 1974.

Smitherman, Geneva. *Black English and the Black Children and Youth.* Center for Blacks Studies, Wayne State University: Detroit, 1981.

Sykes, Cristopher, *Nancy: The Life of Lady Astor.* New York, 1972.

Vine, Phyllis, *One Man's Castle: Clarence Darrow in Defense of the American Dream.* Harper Collins Publishers, 2004

Online Resources:

Fulbright photo:

http://exchanges.state.gov/education/fulbright/fulbbio.htm

http://www.ssunitedstates-film.com/history.html

http://exchanges.state.gov/education/fulbright/fulbbio.htm

Institute of International Education—us.fulbrightonline.org

IVC Detroit - http://www.ivcdetroit.org

Advance Praise for Cal McCray and *Ebb Tide*

"Dr. J. Calvin McCray takes readers on a fascinating journey that is at once international and intimate. It is more than one man's story of a life enhanced by privileges of overseas travel, and, in particular meeting and developing a close relationship with Lady Nancy Astor. It is a solid and sensitive history lesson on the value of education and global and cultural understanding made possible through a Fulbright Fellowship.

"Lady Astor was raised in the American south and went on to become the first woman to serve in England's Parliament. Dr. McCray came of age in Chicago and rose to become a respected educator at a time when blacks rarely excelled in the academic arena. The bond that developed between Lady Astor and Dr. McCray, along with his wife, Vivian, demonstrates what happens when kindness and a quest for understanding take precedence among people of vastly different backgrounds, races, and cultures. It makes for better people and a better world.

"This is a must-read for people interested in history, race relations, and international understanding."

— Cassandra Sprattling, *Detroit Free Press* writer

"Don't miss reading this informative, surprising historical and autobiographical account of Fulbright scholar James C. McCray's experiences in the late 1950s as he and his wife, Vivian, interacted with British royalty in England and on the Isle of Wight.

"Intergenerational benefits will result as young readers see that influential people can and do change positively about other human beings, particularly those of other races, as their experiences enable them to grow and develop. Lady Astor's changes from a sheltered southern-born, traditional American white woman into a welcoming dignitary who voluntarily opened many international doors for the black McCrays are startling. Read the book to learn what the change factors were!

"James C. McCray, born and reared 'up south' in Chicago, and Vivian McCray, born and reared 'down south' in North Carolina were the beneficiaries of Nancy Astor's benevolence, and she was impressed by the personal characteristics of this young black teaching couple."

—   Faustine Jones Wilson, author of *The Changing Mood in America*

"For the past 30 years, Vivian and Cal have been members of IVC Detroit. They are still promoting international understanding by supporting our work on behalf of the International Visitors Leadership Program— an exchange program sponsored by the U. S. Department of State: welcoming dignitaries to Detroit from around the world, breaking down barriers and misconceptions, and promoting an exchange of information between different cultures and countries—one handshake at a time"

— Julie Oldani, Executive Director, International Visitors Council of Metropolitan Detroit

"A very appropriate and rewarding tribute to an icon for all women [Nancy Astor] and a most honorable black female role model [Vivian McCray]. Anyone interested in history, race relations, and international understanding should not miss this story."

— Virgina F. Lewis, Assistant Superintendant, Chicago Public Schools (Retired)

"A gratifying tribute to black women's contributions in the United States."

— Juanita Gonzalez, Montclair, New Jersey, Public Schools (Retired)